ANORAKNOPHOBIA

ANORAKNOPHOBIA

The Life and Times
of a Football Obsessive

ROB GRILLO

First published 2007

STADIA is an imprint of
Tempus Publishing
Cirencester Road, Chalford
Stroud, Gloucestershire, GL6 8PE
www.tempus-publishing.com

British Library Cataloguing in Publication Data.
A catalogue record for this book is available from the British Library.

ISBN 978 0 7524 4561 8

Typesetting and origination by NPI Media Group
Printed in Great Britain

CONTENTS

FOREWORD

by John Helm

As a race we are obsessed with collecting things, hence we hoard everything from piggy banks to obsolete coins, and in sporting terms memorabilia that is completely and utterly trivial, like Polly Ward's autograph or a programme from some obscure North Counties (East) League Cup final. Woe betide the wife who lobs it into the wheelie bin while you're out of the house.

Maybe we are sad, even a little sick, but it's important to cling on to anything that reminds us of events that had a massive influence in formative years.

I've still got the scorecard from my first visit to that delightful old cricket ground at Park Avenue in 1953, when as a schoolboy I squatted down by the boundary ropes to goggle at Lindwall and Miller, and our own hero Len Hutton.

Tragically, my first football programmes from Park Avenue and Bradford City got lost during a house move. I'm still inconsolable, so if that makes me an anorak I'm happy to plead guilty.

Schooldays were more memorable for the back-row quizzes about winning cup-final teams and Ashes captains than anything to do with the Battle of Agincourt or what chemicals to insert in some boring old test tube.

Even now I see grown men walking into lampposts while their minds are on the number of England footballers to have a 'z' in their surname, and people reading newspapers on trains who never get past the sports pages.

We can study the Ryman League table for hours on end and reel off the names of every manager of every football club in the country, but for God's sake don't ask us the name of the Chancellor of the Exchequer or ask us about the FTSE Index.

There are some anoraks who do worry me, like the chap who goes to matches literally every night of the week with the aim of visiting as many grounds as possible – if it's a goalless draw it doesn't count so he has to go again. A pain if it happens at Shakhtar Donetsk!

Most anoraks are harmless individuals who just happen to have fallen in love (passionately) with something which occupies the majority of their daily thinking time – it beats peeling sprouts and takes them on exciting adventures, physically and mentally.

Rob Grillo captures the dilemma of so many of us – how to pursue the passion, retain some level of sanity, and convince the outside world that we're not completely nuts. He does it splendidly.

John Helm
November 2007

PREFACE

As a ten-year-old, I was told that I had an 'unhealthy obsession with football' by one of my schoolteachers, despite the fact that my skills in this department were woefully inadequate. If only that man had known just how true his words would prove to be.

There are all kinds of anorak out there. It is only fair that I write about the ones I know of, the likes of which I like to think I am a truly shining example, so I concentrate here on the sporting anorak and, more specifically, the football anorak. I am no more qualified to write this book than the next geek, but I hope that it is a fair and accurate representation of what one might see, or feel, in the world of the anorak.

Every sport has its followers. Some like to follow their sport obsessively. The same applies to any music genre. There are trainspotters, and even aeroplane spotters, those who spend all day on the buses, anoraks who will seek out every pub quiz within a ten-mile radius in order to demonstrate their prowess, and there is the rather annoying soul who ruins every lecture with his clever and stupidly inappropriate questioning of your favourite lecturer. They are everywhere, and here you will read about several of those involved in sport at grass-roots or non-League level. Except that none of them are annoying.

For you, the reader, it should be a journey of enlightenment. You may see yourself in some of those you read about. You may be an anorak. You will discover that this is nothing to be ashamed of. There again, you may know an anorak, or three. You may feel sorry for them, laugh at them, or even despise them, but you will come to understand that they are maybe not as pathetically sad as you first thought.

This is also my story. It started out as a lonely journey, but has become one that I have shared with a host of other friends and acquaintances, all of them enthusiasts who have taken their pet subject just that bit further.

Throughout this book I refer to the stereotypical anorak as a 'he'. This is not to say that there are no 'she' anoraks out there, so by all means use your imagination when reading of those inside these pages. It has also been my deliberate intention not to belittle or offend anyone in this book. Each and every anorak out there has a sense of humour, just as you do.

There are no mistakes at all to be found in this book. If you should somehow stumble upon some sort of misinterpretation or factual inaccuracy then you will be wrong. I am an anorak and therefore do not make errors of any kind.

ACKNOWLEDGEMENTS

Thanks to Tim Riley, the teacher who initially complained that I had an 'unhealthy obsession with football', and who later became a good friend and teaching colleague of mine! He is living proof that teachers do get it right sometimes.

Every single individual mentioned in these good pages deserves a pat on the back, for their friendship, companionship, honesty, praise, criticism (albeit constructive), for keeping me on the straight and narrow (lets face it, with my parents it could all have turned out so differently) and for basically just being there – you have all played a part in this story! There are others to thank too, such as Wheeze and Darren Holloway, who will be known to the fell-running fraternity in these fair isles.

I do need to single out 'littlest brother' Manny for his adept proofreading of various manuscripts and his honest opinions that were greatly valued throughout, and for his absolute confidence in my ability to get this thing completed. My lovely wife Sue deserves the praise that all husbands who are too preoccupied to help out with the housework need to bestow upon them. She can get her own back now.

Thanks also to Rob Sharman at Stadia books for his continual support and belief in this book.

I also need to acknowledge two demented border collies. Taking Fliss and Fly for a walk twice a day allowed me to clear my head and stop panicking, and allowed new ideas to become far clearer in my mind.

If this book achieves only one thing, it must surely be that the compilation of it has brought back a great deal of good memories for a number of anoraks that I have known. The likes of Ian Robinson and Roy Mason – both of whom you will read about here – were only too willing to relate tales of their past, and both acknowledge that they thoroughly enjoyed looking back and recounting those things of which they are particularly proud. They have their stories, I have mine, and everyone else has theirs, and every one of those memories is priceless.

This book is dedicated to absolutely anybody who may show even the remotest signs of being an anorak. Congratulations and well done.

Enjoy!

Chapter One

THE ANORAK

So precisely who, or what, is an anorak? Contrary to popular belief, anoraks are actually very nice people. This may be something of a shock to an awful lot of people out there, but the stereotypical geek – perceived to be living a drab daily existence – does not exist. The general conception of an anorak as a rather sad and lonely individual, devoid of the social niceties we all take for granted, is just that – a conception. The assumption that he is a rather spotty bachelor, with very little social life and ever fewer friends is a complete misnomer. Spare moments might well be spent online chatting to other anoraks through instant messaging services or internet forums, and life can maybe become a little regimented, but not to the point of being that predictable, and definitely not with the same mundane routine day after boring day.

Look up the definition of the term 'anorak' on the internet, or in your dictionary or encyclopaedia, and you will find plenty of references to the nylon snorkel parka. Some sources refer to the fact that a garment of this type is a trendy item among teenagers. An anorak – trendy? Wikipedia refers to an 'implied excessive interest' taken by a certain individual, aided by an 'intuition that only a geek would wear something so terminally excessive'. So does this then infer that a trendy teenager is a geek, or that a geek is in fact trendy? Mixed messages, methinks.

'Geek' and 'nerd' are just two of the many terms I have seen applied to the stereotypical anorak. This suggests a rather obscurely motivated yet intellectual person. Collector, enthusiast, boring git and tedious person are some of the others. Many other people would offer far less polite descriptions of the much-maligned bloke in the office which I could not possibly repeat here.

There is an alternative and, in fact, widely accepted theory that the term 'anorak' was not first applied to somebody who would be sad enough to wear such a fashion disaster. Seventies disc jockey Andy Archer is reputed to have coined the phrase when referring to the waterproof upper clothing worn by enthusiasts of pirate radio stations that were located offshore in order to avoid being impounded by the authorities. Radio Caroline is probably the most infamous of them all. Scores of avid listeners would sail into international waters in small, inappropriately sized vessels in order to board the transmitting ships and meet their heroes. It is said that the bright colours adorning these individuals were worn to assist the local coastguard, should they have needed rescuing – and there were plenty of examples of that happening.

At least 'anorak' can be used without causing offence to the general public. An alternative moniker for such people was 'wanker'. No joke, you only have to look at the titles of some of the more recent pirate stations that don our airwaves from time to time. How many people have sat in their quiet room taking in the sublime delights of WNKR radio, for instance?

Now, I know many anoraks and not one of them resembles, even slightly, the Roy Cropper-like stereotypical anorak. I am an anorak and I certainly do not resemble that kind of man. For a start, I have never tried to board a pirate-radio ship in the North Sea – or any sea, come to that. The true anoraks of this life are unique professional men – family men; fit, athletic sportsmen with a healthy interest in their chosen sport. They – and myself, in particular – lead perfectly normal lives, enjoy a fruitful yet hectic social life, enjoy meeting people, do have a sense of humour and do not suffer from fashion dyslexia. Designer jeans do NOT look out of place when worn by our good selves, and they complement the trendy shoes and functional and stylish Gore-Tex jackets we so love to step out in.

If you think about it, we could all be part anorak. I am certain that the majority of you reading this book are. It is nothing to be ashamed of. You may not actually consider yourself an anorak but you will share at least one trait that you consider a sure sign of a true, bona fide statto. As you read further, you may discover yourself in these pages. There are more anoraks around than you think, and that is because the large majority of them are no different from every other man or woman in the street. It is just as likely that the well-dressed bloke sat next to you on the bus is an anorak as the shabbily dressed gent with the twitch sat opposite. How do you tell?

Cougar Park may be the erstwhile home of Keighley Cougars Rugby League Club, but it also doubles as the home ground of Silsden AFC of the North West Counties Football League – the competition also embraced by the likes of the Bacup Borough, Salford City and Castleton Gabriels. This is step five in the non-League pyramid, or step nine if you take into account the Premiership and the three Football League divisions. Attendances may just about reach three figures in the North West Counties set-up, but this is the home of the nerd, the geek and the enthusiast.

Let me introduce you to Ian Robinson. Ian is one of the most foremost anoraks in this part of the world. He is more affectionately known these days as 'Lost In Barrow', and there is a very good reason for that. A former Bradford City season-ticket holder, he became disillusioned with the club he had supported since being a child, and given the rise and rise of his local pyramid team decided to give it a go down the road at the famous Lawkholme Lane Cougar Park enclosure.

Ian may never have made it himself in the world of professional sports, but he has a fairly lengthy list of credentials, of which he is proud. At the tender age of sixteen he was the youngest ever person to umpire a match in the Bradford Cricket League, and could well still hold that particular honour. He is a former local football referee. His first game in the middle was Sandy Lane reserves versus Keighley News reserves in the depths of the third division of the Keighley Sunday Alliance League of which you will hear much more later. There was then a subsequent rise in status to Northern Counties East League standard before a lack of fitness (caused by a knee injury, he informs me) forced him out of the game, and thus cut short his visits to the likes of Rossington Main and Pontefract Collieries football clubs. Ian has also served, albeit for only a short time, on the district Football Association committee. Not many people can claim to have done that, the local amalgam of hard-working FA officials never having claimed a particularly fluid membership. There are several very old timers on it, individuals that the local games could not have done without over the past half-century, and there is always a shortage of young, enthusiastic volunteers to assist them in their duties. Ian was that energetic young soul who was happy to answer their call, and it was only through pressure of work that he was eventually forced to pack it in.

Mention Sunday leagues and pub teams in the same sentence and this particular enthusiast will not be happy. Sunday football is serious stuff. He even helped run his local Sunday league team in the early 1980s, working alongside Bradleys FC secretary and friend John Oates during their successful Wharfedale league days. At the time, this league was considered much stronger than the Keighley one, so it was big business as far as Robinson and his co-conspirators were concerned. Besides, as Ian will be at pains to point out, they were no pub side – they were named after a local building firm. There is a difference, allegedly.

What bigger honour is there than to mastermind your local team's victory in the Keighley Sunday Cup final for two years in succession, defeating the mighty Magnet Joinery FC – Keighley's most powerful side for many a year – in the process? This memorable feat is still talked about today around the environs of Crossflatts village – a small commuter settlement at the heart of the West Yorkshire conurbation. Bradley's former pitch is now underneath the new headquarters of the Bradford & Bingley building society. Prince Charles called the old HQ a couple of miles down the road a 'monstrous carbuncle'. Ian Robinson much prefers it to the one at which his side entertained dozens each Sunday morning two decades earlier.

With such fine credentials, it would not be unreasonable to expect this particular gentleman to be a fine, upstanding member of the sporting community. He is. However, he is first and foremost an anorak, and of this he is particularly proud. He is just as liable to offer advice to the man in the middle, or to his trusty assistants, as anyone else in the ground, and having also been a referee's assessor knows precisely which insult to offer.

'You're a right bag of shite you are, you were crap even when you ran the line for me' is a phrase that has been used on more than one occasion in the not very distant past. At times like this, his two lads are prone to moving to another section of the main stand or even disowning him, on the rare occasion that he really does go completely over the top. It has happened.

Despite being sent all over Europe on business when he would prefer to be somewhere else, Ian lives and breathes sport. Mrs Robinson is more than happy to allow him to go to Cougar Park, or to follow his beloved Silsden to the other side of the Pennines, to such far-flung places as Cheshire, Merseyside or even the Potteries. He has the perfect excuse and the perfect alibi: he takes his lads along with him and gives her some much-cherished peace and quiet, or an excuse to engage in much-needed retail therapy. And an awful lot of shopping can be done when the rest of the clan have traipsed all the way to Stoke-on-Trent to see Silsden take on the mighty Stone Dominoes. Therefore Ian has not one, but two other souls with which to share his experiences – two more than the stereotypical single man devoid of any soulmates, living alone with only his books for company.

Mrs Robinson is used to her role as football widow: 'Jean never asks me when I will be home from work or watching sport,' Ian claims. 'That's because I'm prone to go walkabouts.' He's not wrong there. Ask him to pop to the local shop for a loaf of bread and you might have to go and get it yourself. There's a local park between Ian's house and the local corner shop, and if there's a football or cricket match going on then he could be some time.

There is also the locally well-known tale of the father who abandoned his six-month-old son in his pram on the local rec one Sunday. Do you really have to ask who that was? One particularly fine morning, Robinson had taken James on his first trip to Marley playing fields, taking in several games in order to give his first-born child the best experience he could offer on the Sabbath. While spectating on the famous 'tip top' – a set of four pitches based on what used to be a public refuse tip overlooking the rest of the playing fields – it was brought to his attention that a young child was crying in a pram some 200 yards away. Luckily, the match on that particular pitch was able to resume once the errant father had realised that he had indeed had his young son with him at one point that morning. To this day, Jean Robinson is blissfully unaware of these very same facts, and Ian maintains that the correct distance was 'sixty yards, and not a step further'.

These days, James and his younger brother Matthew (or rather 'Lost in Barrow junior' and 'Lost in Barrow junior junior', as they are known in this part of the world) are just as much part of the scene as their father is. In fact, Matthew's tenth birthday party was a real treat for his mates – an afternoon out, all expenses paid, to watch a North West Counties League cup-tie at Cougar Park. Not one of them complained. 'There's one anorak and two half anoraks at our place,' dad quips, and not even Jean Robinson would argue with that.

Away games for the three intrepid sports fanatics are an excuse for a day out, usually on the train. There is no ground too far from a station, and they are not the only ones to travel by this means. Ian has even been known to post rail times on Silsden FC's official forum on the internet, and he reliably informs me that there were fourteen of them on the train to Garforth for a recent FA Vase tie.

Sometimes the three of them decide to go by car, and as his nickname attests, they did indeed once get lost in Barrow. It was a wet and windy Saturday afternoon, and Silsden had an FA Cup preliminary-round tie at Barrow's very own Holker Old Boys. And could they find the ground? Could they heckers like – well, at least not before the game was well past its first half-hour. After all, how many people living in this isolated part of north-west England would be able to direct you to a ground frequented by only the most dedicated followers of the round-ball game? How many people do you know that could direct you to Holker, Cumbria?

Now, I have travelled to away matches with the Robinsons and I can fully understand why and how they got lost – they seem to be so good at it. A short trek across the Pennines to Ramsbottom – a stone's throw from Bury – can turn out to be an ordeal when you have to be there by 7.45p.m. on a Wednesday evening. It's not that Ian isn't a good driver – he is particularly adept in that department – it is perhaps because there are three people trying to navigate at once. The result is that a certain sense of direction seems to be lacking. After all, it isn't that easy to get lost on the way to Ramsbottom. Even Matthew, who is usually quite reserved, has been known to lose his rag on these occasions, while his elder brother is usually the one to calmly find some sense of order while those around him lose their heads.

Not many people can remember places because they have got lost trying to find the football ground there, or have landed there whilst trying to locate the stadium in the adjacent town, but Ian Robinson and his lads do just that. God knows how they first managed to find their way to Squires Gate FC of Blackpool – on time as well – because there are two other floodlit football grounds on the same School Road in the Marton area of the town. They could quite easily have ended up at Blackpool Mechanics or Wren Rovers instead. The three grounds really are on the same street, two of them separated by nothing more than a fence.

Whichever ground they end up at, you can always identify Ian by his rendition of 'Jingle bells, jingle bells, jingle all the way, oh what fun it is to see Silsden win away!' He finds it odd that there are few others willing to join in.

Yet trying to pick Ian Robinson out in an identity parade would be a fruitless exercise. There is nothing outwardly about him to suggest he is an anorak. People used to call him 'ginner' – for obvious reasons – and he was also known as 'Sporting Sam' by his old teammates at Bradleys when he donned his trademark flat cap. That piece of headwear has long been dis-carded, but as he patrols the touchline at some minor Sunday league fixture, Silsden home game or under-10s game at Bingley Juniors (the team that young Matthew turns out for), he could just as easily be a local journalist or referee's assessor as a man with 'an unhealthy interest in football'. In fact, there is nothing unhealthy in his love for the game, in his love for the facts and figures, winners lists, and league tables, and the hundreds and hundreds of football grounds that he has visited either as a fan, club official or man in the middle.

James Robinson is no different from the other lads in his secondary school class. He loves his sport, works hard and lives a perfectly happy, normal existence as a teenager. But rather than worshipping the very ground that the world's best footballers walk on, he is a huge fan of Martin Bland and James Nettleton – not household names, but two lads who do a particularly fine job in the back four for Silsden. Blandy scored the dramatic late goal that saw Silsden promoted in their first ever season in the football pyramid. James Robinson will never forget that because he, his dad and his little brother were all there to see it.

Matthew has been club mascot; he walks round the ground selling fanzines and is prone to standing behind Martin Foulger's goal. Foulger is the club's enigmatic shot-stopping stalwart and Matthew is more then happy to spend forty-five minutes retrieving the ball for his hero. Now he would never be able to do that at Old Trafford, or even at Valley Parade.

These young lads contribute to the Silsden FC fanzine; they are on speaking terms with the manager, the chairman and half of the first team. Along with their dad, they have sponsored the odd home game and have their own spot exactly halfway up the main stand – right in the middle. Their classmates can tell you exactly where Barcelona, Milan and Munich are, but not many of them would have the faintest notion of where on earth Winsford or Ashton-in-Makerfield are. The Robinson lads are anoraks in the making, and every bit proud of that fact.

There is an Ian Robinson, or a Robinson clan, at every non-League ground in the country, and football at this level simply would not pay if there wasn't. We should be thankful for people like them. Long may he, and his lads, be admired.

Like the Robinsons, the nation's favourite BBC statistician, John Motson, is an anorak. He is a minefield of trivia, and useless facts and figures. However, these facts aren't useless or trivial, are they? They serve a purpose. In their correct context they educate us, they give us insight and background information, they tell us the stories behind the unfolding events in any professional football game. Motson does his homework, he is well prepared and knows exactly what he is talking about, yet there is, in essence, very little difference between him and the rest of us out there. Motson is a professional anorak: he is paid to uncover the facts and figures behind each story, and he is an instantly recognisable face and voice on our television screens and radios. If he had been treated with the same disdain as any amateur anorak out there then he certainly would not have made it as far in his profession as he has done.

We can only admire Motson's skills and his dedication, as well as perhaps envy him for making a more-than-comfortable living from what he does best, something that many of us do as a hobby in our own spare time. While it may not be considered complimentary to be called an 'anorak', it is perhaps rather nice to be compared to John Motson, or to be nicknamed

'Motty' at work. If asked, I'm sure John Motson would describe himself as an anorak too; his persona would surely not have stood the test of time had he not continued to provide us with his immense array of useful and relevant facts and figures. After all, how many TV sports personalities have had a computer desktop toy named after them? The 'Mini Motty' is a small windows-based application that allows you to keep up to date with the latest football scores and news headlines for your favourite team. It was only a matter of time before someone jumped on the bandwagon, wasn't it?

There is a story about Motty I really like. He has become synonymous for the wearing of an item just a little different to an anorak – a sheepskin coat. On a recent television programme he admitted that he had actually purchased seven of these from a man in Hornchurch, hoping that they would see out the duration of his television career. They have not been seen quite as much of late, so they obviously haven't.

Among these famous one-liners are three that possibly identify John Motson as a truly great anorak of our time – the tip, the statistic and the historical fact:

'Trevor Brooking's notes are getting wet with the rain. I must lend him some of the Perspex I always bring to cover mine.'

'You couldn't count the number of moves Alan Ball made… I counted four and possibly five.'

'…so different from the scenes in 1872, at the cup final none of us can remember.'

Priceless.

If there is one type of anorak who is often classed, quite wrongly, as being particularly sad in the world of pyramid football then it is the groundhopper – an individual who will visit your local ground not necessarily to see your particular team in action, but with the sole intention of being able to say that he has actually been there. He is essentially there to see the ground, not the team.

Silsden Football Club's home gates were swelled by ground-hoppers during their first season in the world of semi-pro soccer, and there would be phone calls to the club secretary from all corners of the country in the days leading up to each fixture. These calls would consist of requests for directions to the ground, enquiries as to whether a programme would be produced, or questions about the warm food available at half-time. A Saturday morning FA Cup tie saw the gate almost tripled (to well over 300!) as eager travellers from all over the country gathered excitedly for what would be their first visit to a football ground that day. As the final whistle sounded they dispersed to other grounds in the Red or White Rose counties. Some headed towards Manchester, to the Mossleys, Altrinchams and Droylsdens of this world, others in the direction of Leeds and Bradford, in order to sample the fare on offer at Farsley Celtic or Glasshoughton Welfare. Ian Robinson went shopping.

Many groundhoppers see their moniker as a little derisory, and would prefer to be called 'football travellers' instead. Their main sources of information are the superbly unpretentious yet highly informative *Football Traveller* and *Groundtastic* magazines – and yes, they are available by subscription only.

There are differing factions in the world of the traveller, however. Some prefer not to include the ground in their records if the game ends goalless – they will return at a later date, and keep returning until such time as a goal is scored. Pity those then who were witness to a cup-tie at Llanelli rugby club a few years back – the first and only soccer match ever to be held at this particular venue. There was a fair sprinkling of 'hoppers here and they went home without seeing a single goal.

Other travellers care not what the score is, but will revisit a ground if it is rebuilt, or if the uncovered terracing is replaced by a brand-new cantilever stand, or even if the match is abandoned. There are those who will visit a ground twice – once during the day and once under floodlights – and those that must touch one of the crossbars on the pitch before they can tick it off in their little green book.

New grounds are an absolute must, as are those that are about to be bulldozed and replaced by industrial units, car parks, or blocks of sheltered housing. Horton Park Avenue in Bradford probably had more visitors than it had during its Football League years when it was partly built over, its single remaining goalpost and crumbling, weed-ridden terracing adorning the cover of more than one subsequent publication. An indoor cricket academy covered one half of the ground, and the planners and architects who designed it could never have envisaged just how many 'hoppers would photograph it over the ensuing years – not because of any intrinsic beauty it may possess, but merely because it covers part of an old football ground. There must be a lesson to all those football club officials – tell the world that you have sold your ground and they will come flocking through your turnstiles.

Some travellers will not visit grounds below step five on the non-League ladder, while others will strive to visit every known ground in their particular location, mixing with the proverbial one man and his dog on the local rec. I have even met those who prefer to locate the site of a long-defunct football team, their ground gone but not forgotten under-neath the new council car park, or a new housing estate, or even allowed to return to its natural state. Again, there is a publication dedicated to those who wish to follow this route. I'm game for that, although one must remember that in this day and age you can now cheat and visit hundreds of grounds every day if you have Google Earth installed on your home computer. This option is much cheaper too.

In case you have never actually spotted a football traveller before, just look for the chap with the tiny notebook. Every goal is methodically added – scorer and exact time, official attendance, substitutions and/or sendings-off duly noted. If the man on the public address system fails to announce any changes before or during the match then he stands a pretty good chance of being berated for his indiscretions.

There may be more than one of these gentlemen knocking around, in which case take note of the conversation. 'Are you going up to Billingham Synthonia next week? It's an early kick-off, we could fit in the Pickering Town match on the way back.' He may also possess a set of headphones in order to stay in touch with what is happening in the Premiership and Football Leagues, although it is a brave 'hopper who would ever admit to being interested in these fixtures in the first place.

If you were still have problems locating your nearest 'hopper then look no further than the club shop. Not the one that sells programmes and the like, because not all clubs have one, but at the bar, or the burger stand. Pies are big business in this world, and every traveller knows where the largest, tastiest, healthiest, most expensive or most bizarre pie can be found. I discovered that Ashton Athletic FC don't do pies, and word has got round rather quickly. Contrast this with the fare on offer at Bedworth United – faggots, mushy peas and chips – and you can bet that there are a few carriage-loads of 'hoppers travelling there each season to sample them. Rumours spread like lightning: 'Don't know whether this is true or not, but I've head on the grapevine that Rainworth Miners are doing crinkle-cut chips.' Life at the cutting edge.

I am in no position to mock these people – their obsession is far less harmful and far more legal than those of many people I know, and besides, given half the chance I would be at both Billingham and Pickering.

There are other groundhoppers who would not dream of visiting Cougar Park. They may be members of the '92 Club' – a select group of individuals who have visited every one of the ninety-two current Football League and Premier League grounds. Their rules are maybe not as simple as one would expect, though. First and foremost, you must have visited each of the grounds for a competitive home league fixture. This not only excludes friendlies, but also cup-ties and international fixtures. Testimonials are definitely a non-starter.

Also, each and every new ground must be visited, so those who had previously ticked off Doncaster Rovers' Belle Vue enclosure must revisit the town, and in particular the Keepmoat Stadium on Potteric Carr Road in order to keep their status. Nothing controversial there, but should a team lose its Football League status and then return – Carlisle United and Barnet being two recent examples – then these grounds must be revisited. There are more rules: if two clubs should share a home ground then there should be two visits to the venue, once to see each club's home game. If a ground should be redeveloped, or the pitch rotated ninety degrees, then it should also be revisited. Dare I suggest then that some football travellers are groundhoppers, while others are actually club hoppers – or would that be merely confusing the situation further?

Luckily, you do not need photographic proof that you have visited each ground to be in the club, or even references, you are merely asked for a list containing the date of each visit and the official attendance. Easy. Get going.

Of course, there are others who need to go that bit further, hence the '134 Club', for those who have also visited every Scottish League ground as well as the English ones. Others like to include all Conference grounds, viewing this league as an unofficial fifth division, as several sides are fully professional anyway. Others also harbour an ambition to visit every Football League reserve-team venue too. Now that is hard – many use non-League grounds, others may change grounds each season, while some use more than one ground every year. It has been estimated that, should you attempt to compile a league table of most grounds visited by a groundhopper, then you would have to have made your way to roughly 4,000 of them to be anywhere near the top of the list, and in excess of 6,000 to be right at the top. Now that sounds like an awful lot of time, patience, train tickets and pies to me.

I have one particular friend who moved house in order to be closer to Leeds United's Elland Road enclosure a few years back, citing his desire to see regular reserve-team fixtures as the main reason. Gary Kaye is a schoolteacher, a musician and most of all a right anorak. Imagine his surprise then when the club relocated their reserve games to York. It would have been funny had Kaye owned a car at the time. He didn't, and he could not make it to York on public transport in time to see a single fixture, all of which were played midweek.

Gary was also, for a while, made 'Official Poet in Residence' at Elland Road. He appeared several times on local television and radio, reciting his latest offering to the team he has followed all his life, published a complete book of his musings and enjoyed lunch with Ken Bates. Since then his relationship with the powers that be at the club has deteriorated a little and Bates has relieved him of his 'official' duties, mainly due to the opinions he has voiced in some of his verses. This matters little to a man who lives and breathes Leeds United, and who will still be there in his favourite seat should they suffer further hardship in the years to come.

At least you are guaranteed a match-day programme at a Football League venue such as Elland Road. As poor as some of them may be, there are some who will not step inside a non-League ground unless a programme is produced – in effect a souvenir of their visit. Others can get particularly irate if they have sold out before they have reached the ground.

There is a tale of one very unhappy groundhopper who, after travelling halfway across the country, sat in his friend's car in the adjacent car park for the duration of the game upon finding that the club had failed to produce a programme for this particular fixture. His friend enjoyed the game. He was forced to return the following week when, thankfully, a match-day programme was produced.

There are some grounds that the football traveller just cannot reach, unless protracted arrangements are entered into well in advance of the date in question, and I am not talking about the ones on the Western Isles of Lewis and Harris. He can get a ferry or two to those. There are a handful of prison teams in local and regional leagues – Moorland FC in the Doncaster Senior League and Featherstone Prison FC in Staffordshire to name but two. As far as I know, all their fixtures have to be played at home, under strict supervision, and in most cases the eccentric groundhopper is sadly locked out. There are not many people who can complain about not being allowed into prison, but you always have some anorak somewhere who can make that very claim.

I am unable to confirm whether some of the more bizarre claims of groundhoppers are fact or merely fantastical boasting. I have heard the rumour that one gentleman takes a different young lady with him to each hop convention – now he really knows how to show a lady a good time – and I have heard of others who feel it necessary to take a blade of grass from each ground they visit. So what happens if the pitch is relaid? How would they know that Holsworthy FC of the Devon County League had laid new sods if they lived in Cumbria? How would they possibly know the difference between different blades of grass should there be controversy as to whether a pitch had been relaid or not?

There is one particular individual who is often overlooked when travellers discuss at length the grounds they have visited, or the ones they intend to visit in the near future, and that is the much-derided referee. I wonder if any of them consider themselves groundhoppers, after all they do visit an awful lot of football grounds during the season. They could start a brand-new '92 Club', the basic rule being that one must have officiated at each ground on at least one occasion (but would that include a visit as referee's assistant or fourth official?). Referees have made stranger decisions, and some of them could be anoraks in disguise.

On the odd occasion you may find that there are an inordinate number of travellers at a non-League football ground. The home club will usually have been warned in advance that there is a hop going on. This is a tightly organised weekend festival whereby 'hoppers visit as many grounds in a certain area, or league, as can possibly be covered in a set number of days – usually a bank holiday weekend in order to fit in several Monday fixtures. It is the norm for participating clubs to stagger their kick-off times in order to allow their paying customers to get round all of them. After all, it enables each club to earn much-needed extra revenue, and special commemorative badges and shirts are on sale too. Exciting stuff. I hope they remember to order those extra pies.

I could be wrong here, but there seems to be much less of an obsession with visiting grounds of the many other sports and pastimes played in this country. Although I know of some individuals who would visit Odsal Stadium in Bradford three times in order to sample each of the different sports on offer there, there are only a couple I know of who make an effort to visit as many rugby grounds as they can, and this is because they do it in the line of duty. Chris Harte is the charismatic managing editor of the National Sports Reporting Agency and is therefore usually hard at work at these venues. He stands out from the other press hacks because he goes on to write about the grounds he has visited and the people he has met. His books can be hilariously funny, as Harte is not one for officialdom; he is an immensely cheery fellow who expects to be treated in the same polite manner as he would greet you. Woe betide the pompous official who should stand in his way of an afternoon of fulfilment high up in the stands of Britain's sporting venues. It is no surprise that the rugby ground he rates the highest in terms of surroundings, hospitality and basic down-to-earth charm is one set in the heart of the Yorkshire Dales where you are always guaranteed a warm welcome and good food. This is The Avenue in Threshfield, home of Wharfedale RUFC.

Mike Latham, of *The Mighty Bongers* fame, is a good friend and working colleague of Harte's, and is the author of *Rugby League – A Groundhopper's Guide*. There are far fewer major venues to find in this code, but there are some pretty remote village locations that I am sure someone somewhere will be interested in locating. Latham will no doubt have been there first, though.

It is easy to confuse all of this groundhopping malarkey with obsessive compulsive behaviour. Perhaps it is obsessive compulsive behaviour. There again, there is nothing really compulsive about what you, or groundhoppers, do – obsessive maybe, but certainly not something that would make you lose much sleep. If your visit to Shepshed Dynamo has been called off due to inclement weather there's always something else you can do – you certainly won't have problems communicating with others, and definitely won't need to go without food and drink until you finally get round to paying that visit to The Dovecote for their next home fixture a fortnight later. Besides, if a visit to the home of the quaint-sounding Atherton

Laburnum Rovers is cancelled due to the late withdrawal of the match officials, you can quite easily pop across town to the Atherton Collieries versus Salford City fixture instead. And there is always lowly Atherton Town of the Manchester League or Howe Bridge Mills of the Lancashire Amateur League that you could pop in on. The train will take you anywhere, provided the weather hasn't ko'd everything within an eighty-mile radius – and even if it has, there are half a dozen newly purchased books at home you still have to read.

There is another, slightly different breed of anorak, and that's the one that actually competes or takes part in the sport in which they are excessively interested. I say this because I have spent an awfully long time among the fell-running fraternity of this fair isle, and there are some aspects of a normal fell runner's behaviour that are particularly obsessive.

Speak to many runners at your average fell race and you will find that they will tell you they are an anorak, and it is up to you to decide whether or not to believe them.

'We are all anoraks,' Tony Minikin, one particularly sprightly sixty-four-year-old veteran of the sport, tells me as we wade through the knee-deep bogs atop Haworth Moor one wet and windy Sunday morning. 'Put us in a pub together and all we talk about is fell running. We're a set of boring old farts really, who on earth would want to sit with us?'

I can assure you that he really isn't wrong. Should you stray across a set of middle-aged gentlemen in a northern pub, probably bearded and with a sheepdog – most likely called Fly – then you have struck lucky. There are the off-piste training runs to discuss, the long-distance challenges, the dramatic escapes from the clutches of the local swamp, the races run, the wrong turns, the abject failures, the incident with the farmer, and a host of other wild and wacky tales that the majority of the population care very little about.

The tales get longer and more far fetched as the beer flows, but very few are actually made up. They may bore the majority of the population rigid but once you have been touched by the hand of the fell runner you may never look back. Take Richard Askwith, for example, a London-based journalist who became smitten with the sport and the challenges it provided (the Bob Graham Round, to be exact – a long-distance, high-level Lake District challenge that is the ambition of virtually all fell runners to complete within twenty-four hours at some point in their lives). Askwith went on to document this obsession, penning the award-winning book *Feet in the Clouds: A tale of Fell Running and Obsession*. Other established and well-known names in the world of fell running have written books on their long-distance feats, and you can be sure that the majority of the thousands who take part in the sport have read them. Joss Naylor has been featured on many a TV programme in the north of England. The Lake District's favourite son, he may not be the most famous British sportsman in history, but among the fell runners of this world he is a hero – revered and much loved by all – who will never be equalled.

There seem to be few under forty in the sport these days, partly because there are fewer youngsters continuing past their teens – which, of course, is currently a problem in all sports – but also because forty seems to be the age when an awful lot of people decide to try out the sport for the first time. Fatal. Mid-life crisis or not, once you have tried it there seems to be very little chance of you ever letting it go.

The sport takes over your life. You keep a spare smelly, sweaty kit and trainers in the boot of your car should you wish to tackle the nearest mountain when you stay with relatives. Every waking hour is spent thinking about the next run: when will you fit it in? How long should you give yourself? When should you eat? What should you eat? Do I need the toilet now or later? This most certainly is obsession. I should know. You do not need to be a world-class fell runner to be totally obsessed with the sport, you do not need to be a champion to train every day, no matter what the weather is like, over hill and dale, and you do not need any talent at all to be able to fit in over 100 miles a week. You just need the will, an awful lot of time, and a really understanding partner. There again, I know so many fell-running couples that it is obvious the sport takes over the family itself.

Some would argue that the fell runner isn't an anorak at all. I would disagree. It is one of those seriously and dementedly obsessive sports you can share with your husband/wife/partner too, whether they are also taking part or standing, shivering their arse off on the side of a remote hill with a thermos flask and chocolate digestive, wishing you would just hurry up so that they can get back in the car, where the dog is getting rather impatient and is on the verge of chewing the steering wheel.

There are the Munroe baggers – those who just have to tackle all of Scotland's 3,000-metre peaks – and those who just have to tackle every one of Britain's long-distance challenges, and then tackle them all over again in order to do them faster. It does not matter how many pairs of shoes he gets through, how many family members are waiting on that hillside (because they chose to be there) or how many hours of well-earned holiday are being used up – these things just have to be done. This fanatic has every single Ordnance Survey map pertaining to his challenge, maps at each and every scale. They have been scrutinised time and time again – and then again in order to check the route, the terrain, and the location of the local hostelry at the close of day. Every spare weekend will have been spent training, organising and reccying the route. Training partners will have been cajoled into doing 'that bit in the middle where the trail gets a bit vague in places'. Jelly Babies and Kendal Mint Cake are his staple diet for the duration of his effort, and his workmates worry about him because he is looking gaunt. This means he is at the peak of his fitness – the masses will never appreciate that fact, nor will they understand what pleasure could ever be derived from running over hill and dale, through endless bogs, knee high tussocks, up and down, up and down again, and then up and down the next hill. And for what? In order to get to the other side.

One famous tale doing the rounds refers to a fell-running fanatic of a different type. This particular chappie, hailing from the north of Wales, would get to nearly every race in the area, either competing or photographing the runners, but was also something of an environmentalist. He became increasingly concerned with footpath erosion and the impact on the larger fields of 500 or so runners on virgin hillside. In order to test his hypothesis that such an impact would cause damage, he chose a bit of suitable fell near his house and, donning his best new fell-running shoes, proceeded to pound up and down the same track 1,000 times! He took photographs before and after his efforts and, to his great surprise and chagrin, could see no visible difference! Such a noble and valiant but ultimately pointless exercise surely propels this would-be eco-runner firmly into the upper reaches of geekdom?

Shaun Denham from Leeds – another middle-aged gent truly addicted to the sport – would agree with Tony and myself. His wife truly believes he is a geek:

> She says the very fact that over 100 of us spend hours posting on our internet forum every night is proof alone.
>
> I did try to give her some history into our fine sport. No joy there either. I said that the first marathon run was by Pheidippides and that it was basically a fell run. I pointed out that he was a soldier and not a geek. The wife just said he was Greek and that's only one letter away from being one anyway.
>
> We even have a section within our website forum devoted to the suitability of anoraks. As soon as anyone posts anything asking for advice on the best type to have there are a multitude of postings, each giving line and verse about their particular favourites best attributes. Taped seams, storm flaps, wired hoods, Gore-Tex, Paclite, Featherlite, Pertex.

He is perhaps a little harsh on himself when he suggests that there is an inverse relationship between sporting prowess and anoraknobility, as one might put it. Denham is far from being a back marker in local fell races as he claims, although it is hard to argue against the fact that among fell runners he is something of an obsessive. It is true that many anoraks are merely frustrated sportsmen, but you need only to look in the direction of the sport's greatest achievers, such as Hugh

Symonds – who made the first continuous traverse of 303 mountains of Britain and Ireland – to see that even the best of us can be particularly obsessive and geeky when it comes to sheer bloody mindedness in achieving one's goal. The football anorak is very different to the fell-running anorak, but that same single-minded pursuit of a goal, whether accepted by others or not, makes them likely bedfellows.

Working in the world of IT, Denham is able to offer a little insight into to what made him the man he is today:

> As a kid, when all teenage boys had pictures of semi-clad women all over their walls, I had the Ordnance Survey Geological Map of the British Isles on mine. My love of maps has continued. I'm sure the missus would love me to have copies of Penthouse in the downstairs loo these days instead of the Fell Runners Association magazine, now that really does bore her. Working in IT doesn't help the cause. Especially when I end up putting all my race maps into my Anquet software.

He concludes, 'My definition of an IT geek is someone who is fluent in Linux. The fact that I know what Linux is, in my wife's eyes, makes me a geek. I cannot argue with that.' Not many people would want to argue with that.

Others would be seriously concerned at the bedroom habits of fellow fell runners. Denham is not alone in 3D map building with his duvet. Forget the latest digital mapping techniques, the idea here is to try to form the shapes of the hills you are soon to run up by closely studying the contours on your Ordnance Survey map. This is taking DIY to extremes, if that's what it really is. I think it was Billy

Connolly who preferred the 'my God, I was just trying to get rid of a large spider from the bed' approach when caught indulging in something that should have been kept a little more discreet.

You don't necessarily have to do your thing on the fells and mountains of this good land to be a bit nutty. Take the road runner who, the night before any race, would take a stroll around the route and carefully remove all debris from the road and pavement in order that he may not be impeded in his efforts. He is also said to take snapshots of each water-stop area and paint white markers along the route, probably to remind him to look at his stopwatch. I have still to hear a decent explanation as to why the photographs need to be taken, though – unless some time in the future I come across a book entitled *Great Water-Stops I Have Known*, and then I will know why.

Now consider the fell runner who fell over his lace and badly broke his arm high up on the Brontë moors while doing what he enjoyed most on the first day of his holiday. It would have been so easy for him to flag down the nearest car on the nearest road, or to knock on the door of the closest farmhouse in order to seek help. But no, the two-hour training run had to be completed; there was no excuse for not running those final five miles home. After all, it was a bright sunny day, he was feeling strong and, other than a bloodied knee, his legs were in ship-shape condition. So he did run home, right past his wife's place of work, with bemused motorists travelling in the opposite direction wondering why on earth some bloke with a broken arm was trotting merrily on his way. This is obsession, beyond the call of duty for the normal man, but not for a fell runner. You do not let broken limbs stop you, and yes, it is worth having a bath and cleaning oneself up first before waiting for the wife to come home to ferry you to hospital. I was proud of myself for doing that. Mrs Grillo was not amused.

As a final point, I would argue that, even if an anorak was, officially, a sad, boring geek, then this would not necessarily be a terminal issue, unless of course he was to actively engage in some dementedly stupid activity. As far as I am aware, nobody has died simply because they took an interest in a sport (rather than competing in it), choosing to visit a brand new football ground, for example, or deciding to walk all the way up the hill to Tow Law Town's stadium in the north-east.

American medical studies are purported to have proved decisively that the actual wearing of an anorak, rather than merely behaving like one, could prove terminal, though. The Royal Society of Medical Press reported recently that from a study sample of roughly six healthy volunteers, wearing a total of four different types of anorak, they were able to conclude that those who wore theirs with the hood up were more likely to be hit by a moving vehicle while crossing the road. They explain that this is solely due to the fact that vision is impaired by said hood, and advise that anyone wearing an anorak should 'turn to look sideways before crossing the road'. Well knock me senseless.

Chapter Two

AN ANORAK IN THE MAKING

I suppose I wasn't much different to all the other kids at school. I thought that I would one day stand out from the crowd. Nobody else had an inkling that I was going to stand out, I just knew it. Little did I know that every single other boy and girl at Grange juniors thought that about themselves too.

It could have started when my old man took me trainspotting at weekends, thereby unintentionally contributing to a subsequent 'unhealthy interest' in statistics – seemingly irrelevant sports statistics. There again, that doesn't seem to have affected my brother Charles, a little under two years my junior, who was equally at risk of developing the same obsessive traits. I never actually set out to be an anorak, there was no life-changing decision or single defining moment that led to my immersing myself in a complete and overriding world of facts, figures and minute statistical information, the type that the majority of the population would consider irrelevant and pointless.

Maybe it was because there was a long list of numbers in each trainspotter's handbook – of which there were a couple of new editions every year to keep me busy. One book listed the entire stock of registered multiple units, both operational and defunct – not the kind of thing you explain to a girl on your first date. I don't actually remember much about the trains I saw – *Mallard* and the *Royal Scotsman* come to mind – or the platforms I stood on, or which stations I actually visited, or even whether I actually enjoyed myself much. But it must have been fun, if only because it was a day out with dad, and there are remarkable links that can be drawn between this and my subsequent obsession with anything that involved lists, data, statistics and meaningful facts.

So how many of us would admit at a job interview or first date that we once stood on a remote station platform collecting train numbers in our dim and distant past? Not many, I would imagine. If only there were more lie detectors in use.

My home town has never been the most outstanding of places, pretty average really, but not half as bad as the book *Crap Towns* would suggest. It has never really been the same since the textile mills shut down, followed not long afterwards by the engineering works that went into terminal decline. Few people would have heard of Keighley, West Yorkshire, were it not for its steam railway and its close proximity to the Brontë village of Haworth, itself a pretty uninteresting place were it not for the famous parson and his even more famous literary daughters (and one alcoholic son). However, it was, and still is, the area I grew up in and for many reasons the majority of us here are proud of it.

If I wasn't any different to all those others around me, I liked to think that at least my hobbies and interests were different from those of my mates and two little brothers – all three of us were particularly bright yet hopelessly inept in our earliest sporting exploits. I had no idea at the time that in the big wide world there were others who were just like me. I happily played at cops and robbers with the other kids (our version of one particular American detective series was Starsky and Starsky, because no one ever wanted to play Hutch), and I had no problems fitting in at school, but Mr Timothy Riley, that primary school teacher who described my interest in football as 'unhealthy', was spot on. I was different, and this is how…

Perhaps rather oddly, there was not one person in my family who shared even the remotest interest in football with me, at least not when I was a kid (my youngest brother, Manny, did develop the taste in later years). I was hooked, and I quickly decided that I was going to be a superstar. I would grace Wembley's hallowed turf and it was inevitable that I would score a dramatic last-minute winning goal in the World Cup final. That was no different to the dreams of hundreds of thousands of pre-pubescent youngsters – there were several lads knocking around in my class at school who had far more potential than I did – but there was a much deeper love of the game that was slowly emerging.

As it turned out, there was only one thing that stopped me from becoming one of Britain's best-known and well-loved footballers, and that, unfortunately, was my astonishing lack of ability. I really was a poor footballer, and still am. I kept goal for my school soccer team a couple of times, but only because my PE teacher felt sorry for me. Once I got to secondary school I never had a chance of making even the third team. Not that this has ever prevented me from becoming an expert in the field of irrelevant football statistics – and here I am not only referring to the round-ball game, but also rugby league, rugby union and, come to think of it, practically any sport that contrives to produce a myriad of statistically mind-boggling information (mind-boggling to the uninitiated, that is).

As a ten-year-old I could happily discuss at length the previous weekend's First Division results. Tony Currie and Ces Podd were two of my heroes, and from the comfort of my armchair I admired the skills of Sheffield United's Argentine recruit Alex Sabella on Sunday's *Football Special* on Yorkshire Television. The 1980s were dawning: out went the hideous sideburns and in came the glamour perms adorned by the likes of Terry Curran of Sheffield Wednesday. It was as if he was on local TV all the time. I loved that videprinter on *Grandstand* and now and again would do the unthinkable – I would watch the videprinter on Dickie Davies' *World of Sport* instead. Despite the presence of their silver-haired presenter, ITV's offering was a shoddy alternative, save for the odd wrestling bout from Keighley's salubrious Victoria Hall.

I was no different to many others in this respect, but those very same weekends I did something that no other kid in my form at Grange Junior and Infant School shared a passion for. It may have been a half-mile trek to the nearest newsagents, but Sunday mornings were something special. I already knew that Leeds United had underperformed, that Bradford City had once again contrived to snatch defeat from the jaws of victory, and that Liverpool had again stolen a march on their rivals for the League title. There was something else that would demand my attention, and it wasn't my cherished Dennis the Menace fan-club badges and secret passwords.

Scouring through the results pages of Sunday's *News of the World*, my eyes focussed further down the page on the tiny results section below the four Football Leagues tables. I was more concerned with the Worsbrough Bridge Miners' Welfares of this world, and I eagerly sought out Emley and Winterton Rangers' results in the old Yorkshire League. Not many years later, I was gutted when the league merged with the Midland League to form the Northern Counties East League. You may not have cared, but I did. In an era when many school kids were utterly confused when faced with the Central League – a competition solely for the reserve sides of Football League teams – I knew at an early age that any effort to introduce my classmates to the coming and goings of the Yorkshire League would only be met with derision, ridicule and disdain. I was also deeply anxious that there was no team from sunny Keighley listed in these results. As far as I was concerned, famous teams came from other places; Keighley had somehow been missed out.

Of course, in those days there was no internet, and local soccer results on Ceefax were a long way off, so the Sabbath revolved around getting up early and dashing off to Whitakers' newsagents in Stockbridge to glean the minor-league results involving the likes of Frecheville Community Association, Denaby United and Yorkshire Amateurs. Some Sunday papers even carried the West Riding County Amateur League results – that really was a bonus, as I would only ever see the other Sunday papers if we had visitors, or if there was an old copy in the dentist's surgery or on the teacher's desk.

I had not the faintest notion that there were others out there who would share such interests. I could talk about trains with the old man (when I was lucky enough to see him on the odd weekend), and could quite easily discuss the weekend's First Division fixtures with my mates. But who on earth would ever want to know whether Leeds Ashley Road had won at Harrogate Railway Athletic or not, or whether Rawmarsh Welfare had managed to climb away from the foot of the table? I didn't really care that the majority were blissfully unaware that these teams even existed as I didn't particularly want to share such interest with my family or friends – it was my interest, my hobby. I may not have had much money, or been particularly good at sport, but I could read about it, I could immerse myself in something that my peers were either oblivious to, or otherwise cared little for, something with which I could escape the real world, and a climate of bitter divorce and recriminations.

And then there was Subbuteo, or rather Martin Butterfield had Subbuteo. I had some other table-football game that had literally fallen off the back of a lorry. It wasn't a patch on Subbuteo, but it was my footy game and nobody else had one like it. Recticel had manufactured it and the players were a little scrawny. They fell to pieces after a few weeks, due mainly to my clumsy hands, and I had to paint them myself. This task I performed particularly badly, but the Recticel football game at least enabled me to take the next steps towards my little-known goal of becoming a bona fide anorak.

Most junior-school kids would be happy with the odd challenge match against their mates or their dads, but in my case it went further – much, much further. There was, of course, the occasional challenge match – Master Butterfield was within moments of a resounding 19-1 flicking victory at his house one night, his inevitable victory spurned only by his dad, who took slight exception to the hysteria downstairs that had woken him at three in the morning. The game was declared void and never replayed.

There was much more to this lark than that, though. Within weeks I had organised the '1978 Robby Grillo Football League', and it consisted of ten teams, all of whom played home fixtures on my big green mat. The usual suspects were involved – Manchester United, Liverpool and the like – plus Wrexham and Bradford City, City because they were the local, albeit unsuccessful, Football League team and Wrexham because Dai Davies played for them. Davies was a damn fine goalie, and once managed to get himself sent off in front of the *Match of the Day* cameras for manhandling the referee. I liked him for that and therefore Wrexham deserved to be included. As homework increasingly took a back seat, the Grillo league championship was followed by another, and then another, with all fixtures and results diligently recorded in an old school maths exercise book I had supposedly lost. All fixtures were played in the Recticel stadium in the evenings and matches were usually ten minutes each way. There was no one else involved, I played one team and I played the other, there was no need for any other involvement, and I certainly didn't want to share my league with anyone else, except Martin Butterfield. It was important that he was kept fully up to date with proceedings, so every other evening we would 'phone in' our results. He also ran his own league, so it was only natural that I should be party to this too. It was only years later that I realised that this most serious of tasks had caused much amusement for our parents.

My good friend had another advantage over me – he had a typewriter. I had a pen I had nabbed off my mum, and so my results sheets were much less professional. I got his old score-board for free when his dad bought him a new, ultra-classy one that really looked the part. Even then, there were signs that my obsession for the most minute of details could take a turn for the worse. The scoreboard had with it a plethora of team name cards, one of which was ES Clydebank FC. I knew that there was a Clydebank, and an East Stirling, the latter not appearing on the team cards, so I was confused. The world of mergers, amalgamations and takeovers was still a little beyond me, and again it was a good few years before I fully appreciated the furore this short-lived name had caused.

Eventually, these real-life teams were supplanted by those from the depths of Rob Grillo's imagination. 'Recticel Rangers' and 'Grillo's Gallopers' were leading lights in the competition, there was a pyramid of promotion and relegation years before the FA introduced it to the non-League game, and there were cup competitions and a 'European Cup' to compete for. Grillo's Gallopers eventually supplanted Leeds United as leading team in the competition, achieving no less than five successive league and cup doubles, and giving rise to the suggestion that maybe I was not as impartial as I had thought during these competitions.

What is important about this early chapter of my life is not whether Wrexham avoided the wooden spoon, or whether my friends had better football games than I had, but the fact that I took my game so seriously, and from it evolved a whole host of useless statistics and mundane facts that only I could really understand or take an interest in (Martin Butterfield excepted, of course, and he grew out of this phase of his life much quicker than I did). I certainly had no idea that Subbuteo itself was a global game and that there were hundreds of thousands of enthusiasts all over the world, the elite few competing for British, European and World titles. If I had known, I'm sure I would have talked at least someone in my wider family into buying it for me, although it would not have changed the fact that I would have been crap at the game, and there would have been no last-minute abandonment when suffering a 19-1 drubbing in real competition.

In these formative years I also witnessed my introduction to the real thing itself, specifically the Keighley Sunday Football Alliance. The town's premier round-ball competition was, and still is, almost exclusively based around the (in)famous Marley playing fields on the eastern edge of the town, right in the middle of the river Aire's flood plain, and – interesting if you are a geography student, or teacher – adjacent to the confluence of the rivers Aire and Worth, two watercourses that have claimed many a match ball through the years.

Marley, consisting of nearly a dozen rugby and soccer pitches, is easily the most important sporting venue in the history of this fairly average West Yorkshire town. There is not a single person among the 50,000 or so residents of Keighley who cannot claim to have stepped foot on these grounds at least once in their lives.

Pitch number four hosted all the home games of Juventus Football Club. Yes, Juventus, but not THAT Juventus. This bunch of first- and second-generation Italian immigrants had begun life as AC Alassio, their name a combination of the titles of a local coffee house and a particularly successful Serie A side.

Following their change of moniker, they had the dubious honour of being the first team that I actually supported or followed. My reason for choosing this particular agglomeration of pretty average footballers was merely that the stepfather I happened to have at the time – a certain Alfonso Grillo – was an Italian hairdresser, and a couple of the lads he employed turned out for Juventus every week. They, like the rest of the team, displayed the same amusing and highly dramatic Mediterranean temperament, both at work and at play. It did bother me that Alfonso himself did not turn out for this lot because he assured me that had recently retired from playing for his village club, Alife, in the Italian fifth division. He even took me to see their home ground during a visit to Italy so of course he could not possibly have been lying. I suspect that I may have been conned there as I have since done a bit of research into this Alife FC and the supposed Italian fifth division.

Back in sunny Keighley, Juventus were very real, and very Italian in every respect. Every victory was celebrated as if it were another World Cup final success. In the beginning they all aspired to be Roberto Bettega or Franco Causio, and they would all have made excellent goalkeepers as they had been able to dive far better than Dino Zoff ever could. Then, in 1982, they all wanted to be Paulo Rossi, the original bad-boy-come-good role model. Each goal was celebrated in Marco Tardelli style, arms outstretched and head shaking with sheer euphoria as if they had just netted that second goal in the final against the Germans. The Keighley Sunday Alliance loved them for it.

I got a clout off my dear mother when I first suggested popping down to Marley one Sunday morning to watch the team play – after I had finished scouring the minor football results in the *News of the World*. I think I actually got sent to bed for being cheeky. Anyone with any sense knew that Juventus didn't play down the road at Marley, they played in Turin and did not share their huge stadium with the likes of Keighley Grinders or Burlington Arms FC. Years later I did get that apology, by which time Juventus had sadly folded, playing as Villa Roma FC in their final campaign when a local restaurant sponsored them, and in total lasting a mere decade, which is about the norm for your average Sunday parks team.

I had experienced instant success with my new mates who, as runners-up in the second division behind Shoulder of Mutton FC, were promoted in my first season of following them. The following year they nearly won the first division, but their subsequent slide down the league ultimately led to an ageing team losing interest and moving onto something less physically demanding instead. Several of them, I understand, moved on to selling ice creams to young kids outside the local schools, while the others continued their days jobs as car mechanics, window cleaners and regulars at William Hill bookmakers.

So, by the time I was barely into my teens I was undeniably hooked on the trials and tribulations of what was essentially a pub team. They didn't cheat, although, with the typical Italian temperament, they played hard and suffered their fair share of disciplinary blemishes. They had a jolly good time playing in the Italian national team kit, and they were able to cunningly 'import' players from better sides in other leagues if they had an afternoon kick-off. Therefore the great Keith Lowe of Magnet Joinery FC, one of the country's premier Sunday works teams, would often turn out for a second game with Juventus and he became my first real idol. Ian Greenwood was his mate; he also turned out for Juve and even fitted a new central heating system in my house. To me, it was the equivalent of what would be Wayne Rooney or David Beckham coming for tea. He also fancied my cousin. Imagine that.

I know that Greenwood and Lowe are not exactly the typical Italian gentiluomo, but you have to remember that they did service the boilers in the homes of many Italian families around town, which qualified them to play for the 'Azzurri'. Besides, they were good footballers too, and that speaks volumes in the Keighley Sunday Alliance. Few could have mourned the team's passing as I did.

There was also Mark Burns. For a brief period as a supporter of Keighley's Juventus FC I would come across Mark, who fulfilled an almost identical role as sole supporter of his local Sunday side. So for a short while I had someone with whom to share my Sabbath-day ritual, in the same way that Martin Butterfield had shared my passion for irrelevant invented football leagues. Mark supported Parkwood United. They used to be called Broom United, allegedly because their founder member lived on the appropriately named Broom Street. Juventus pipped them for promotion, but Parkwood gained revenge in a bruising league cup encounter, and Mark went on to appear in the sports pages of the *Keighley News* even more than I did.

We would position ourselves directly opposite any photographer we could spot at Marley. This would inevitably result in either one or both of us having to briefly leave our respective Sunday league games to have our mugshots taken for the back page of the local press, celebrating a decisive strike or passively observing a controversial moment in a top-of-the-table Lord Rodney versus Timothy Taylors clash. Fame. It was a particularly sad game we played, but it kept us happy, and at least we weren't hanging about the streets breaking into the cars or setting light to garden sheds. Alas, it was then Mark's turn to find something better to do on a weekend, and I was on my own again.

This is what being an anorak is all about. You don't need the support of friends or family. You do not need to be able to share your passion with the ones you love, or with your best mates (although it is a bonus if there is, albeit briefly, a Martin Butterfield or Mark Burns with whom you can share this obsession). You don't even need to be accepted. What is important is that you gain that sense of pride, that satisfaction in the knowledge of the tiniest fact that others may or may not seek, or the warm glow felt inside when your local Sunday team comes from 3-0 down to win 4-3 in driving wind and rain in front of no one but you.

Having my picture taken standing behind a goalpost in the local park wasn't the start of an obsession with my local newspaper, however. I was already pretty well established there. Not that this was due in any way to any talent I had for a particular sport. Having finally come to the conclusion that I was never going to grace Wembley – or even the Marley centre pitch – I had decided to become a top athlete along the lines of Sebastian Coe and Steve Ovett instead. They were never out of the news, and I wanted some of that success too – surely it couldn't be that hard. Unfortunately, but not surprisingly, a distinct lack of athletic success in my early years mirrored my experiences on the football field. At least I was trying, and in later years I did get quite good at running. Honest.

The world of schoolboy football did make me a hero on my street and in my class at school. Not having made the Grange under-11 team for a game at Oakworth, I was persuaded to write about it instead. And this was where the influence of one person made all the difference.

Rod Farnell was revered by all around him: his teaching colleagues, the parents who went along to help him run the myriad of sporting teams he organised and, most of all, the kids he taught. These were the days when PE teachers had the time to organise sports fixtures for Saturday mornings. Most of us over the age of thirty will remember Saturday mornings for that very reason. He had games to organise every weekend during the football season – or at least it seemed that way – and his enthusiasm held no bounds. Farnell's infectious personality and love for sports rubbed off on his football, rugby, cricket and athletics teams, all of which had more than their fair share of success, and it was because of this that we forgave him for smoking his trademark pipe on the touchline. He knew I was a hopeless footballer, that I would never make an ace goalscorer or particularly fine goalkeeper, and he was well aware that I was only ever a pretty average runner. But he knew that, compared with most of the other kids in my class, I was pretty good at writing. After all, he was my class teacher too. 'Why not write a report on the game instead?' he suggested, perhaps noticing that tear in the corner of my eye after I had once again failed to make the team for the next match. So I did. Encouraged to do so by Farnell, I sent the report to the *Keighley News*, which was 'read by nine out of ten local households'. So could this make me famous instead?

What happened next did, in fact, change everything. 'Introducing our newest reporter' proclaimed the back page in large bold type the following Friday. My work, as poor as it was, had been printed in its entirety and, probably because there was not much else to report on the back page that week, I was centre stage in the sports pages of the local broadsheet. I had to stand up in assembly. The head declared that I was a credit to the school. I had made it as far as I was concerned, utterly famous within my own classroom and on my own street, and this time there was no one to tell me that I had merely an 'unhealthy obsession'. I had started, I had found acknowledgement for something I actually rather enjoyed, I had combined my love of sport and trivia, and of the written word, and I certainly wasn't going to finish there. And I didn't finish there because over the next few years I won the *Bradford Telegraph & Argus* 'junior journalist of the year' competition not once but twice. All I had to do was design a made-up newspaper, easy for a lad like myself, by now fast approaching geekdom.

My contributions to the local newspaper were collected in what became the first of many scrapbooks, which eventually covered a range of sports. I was referred to as a 'roving reporter' – probably because the editor of the *Keighley News*, John Liddle, was far too polite to call me a 'sad anorak' – and I covered the top sporting events in the region. I was there when the World Steel Strand Pulling Championships were held in a local village hall. My cousin finished third in the under-14 boys event and, strangely, there were very few contestants from outside the White Rose county that took part that day.

My enthusiasm held no bounds and for the first time in many I completely overstepped the mark, such was my desire to do everything at once and in the shortest possible time span. I accosted the local sporting hero, Olympian Steve Binns – at the time the World junior record-holder for 5,000 metres on the track – in the local sports shop where he worked part-time. He was to be the first sporting superstar to be interviewed by this up-and-coming young upstart. Quietly spoken, Binns was far too polite to refuse and was thus subjected to all manner of inappropriate and juvenile questions from a young man who hadn't a clue what he was doing. Liddle was forced to point me in the right direction, no doubt a little embarrassed by now.

At least I had interviewed the most important sporting celebrity in the universe – in my eyes anyway – and as I aspired to become just as successful a distance runner as he was going to be (as well as by now becoming the world's most renowned journalist) then it was entirely appropriate that I should approach him in this way. I had it all mapped out. Easy. I fear that I was not the most impartial of commentators – the swine who bullied me at school was guaranteed to get the worst write-up every week, and the weekend he scored two own goals in a school football match was the weekend I devised my most thorough and complete masterpiece to date. I enjoyed seeing him squirm as the head teacher, as per usual, read out my contribution to the local broadsheet in morning assembly. I may not have been physically the strongest of lads, but I could cause the type of aggravation that lasted much longer and reached a far wider audience than a black eye ever could.

Without the confidence instilled in me by Farnell – who passed away at far too young an age, just days before I had my first book published – I may never have pursued my interest in writing, and of all the people I have ever met, he stands out as the single biggest influence in what I have achieved subsequently. Not everyone I know would thank him for that.

Despite leading a pretty normal life, I was still in my own world once home, and there was one other thing that set me aside in my formative years. Most lads of my age turned to cricket in the summer months. I didn't. For a start, I was an even worse cricketer than I was a footballer, and I cannot stress just how inept I was at the latter. Plus, I didn't particularly enjoy watching, playing, or studying facts about cricket, even if my junior school were national six-a-side champions (thanks to Rod Farnell as usual).

Instead, as Frankston Pines, Fawkner and Dandenong City replaced Liverpool and Manchester United on the football pools, the world of the Australian soccer league opened up to me. I knew that South Oakleigh were a team of Greek immigrants, and that Chelsea and Brighton were struggling Victoria League teams. Not one other person at school or at home gave a damn. There was Acacia Ridge and Bundaberg in Queensland, Burnie, Somerset and Leven in Tasmania, Azzurri in West Australia, another Azzurri in South Australia, and Juventus in Victoria state – another Juventus! There was no way I could make their home games on time every weekend. I collected Aussie league tables, I wrote off to the *News of the World*, *The Sun* and the *Daily Mirror* for final tables, league compositions and team-name changes, all provided by the press agencies of that time. They sent me them: some were wrong, but I had a grand old collection from the early 1980s. Unfortunately, I was less adept at predicting the scores of their matches, otherwise I would be living a life of luxury in the middle of a grand estate on a remote Scottish island.

I have no idea where all this information went. I have moved house that many times that they undoubtedly got thrown away with the rubbish one year. I never knowingly throw things away, I am a hoarder, and if I throw anything away I may find I need it later. The Aussie final tables were priceless, and it was these that undoubtedly triggered my obsession with final league tables. Here we are talking final league tables of any kind; whether it be the Craven & District Football League, the Crosshills Snooker League or the Pennine Amateur Rugby League, I have to have a record of them. I have scrapbooks full of final tables. The more recent ones are now backed up on disc. Even incomplete final tables are acceptable; even they have their uses – uses to nobody but me. If you want a full set of Keighley Sunday Alliance tables, I'm your man.

Australian final league tables were intriguing. It's no wonder I became obsessed with them. It wasn't so much the number of points gained that year, or the number of goals conceded or matches drawn, but the teams themselves. The figures were irrelevant, the teams weren't. Why had the team that finished in fourth place in the West Australia State League been demoted two divisions? Two teams had changed names in the fourth division of the Queensland League, but which team was which? Why didn't Somerset get promoted to the Tasmania State League North after their runaway success in the North East division the season before? And where the hell were such places as Mooroolbark, Nunawading and, er, Chelsea, Brighton and Enfield? Teams disbanded, others merged, others disappeared into oblivion, but in an era when you could only find out about these things in the newspapers (and from their sports editors when you wrote to them) these were big questions for a young lad intent on finding the answers somewhere.

As I grew into my teens, I encountered the usual distractions from the world of sporting facts and figures. Greenhead Grammar School provided those very distractions. (I am reminded of my every day as a pupil there because I now teach in that very same establishment. It may now be a 'high school', but for the time being it remains on the same site as that which shaped my future years.) O-levels, geography, girls and the top-forty singles chart dominated (not necessarily in that order). Jennifer Beals replaced *Charlie's Angels* star Jaclyn Smith as top totty, and one day I would meet her, settle down and live happily ever after. I would still, however, pursue my career as world-class athlete and world-renowned journalist. At least it was supposed to work like that. Some time during my second year at Greenhead, Beals was unceremoniously dumped in favour of Bananarama's dishy brunette, Karen Woodward. Sadly, we were never to meet, she missed her chance too. She had to make do with settling down with Wham's Andrew Ridgeley instead.

You would have thought that I would have been the first to enrol on the school's sports studies CSE course at Greenhead, organised and taught by my quite brilliant head of year, former Wolverhampton Wanderers trialist Stuart Jackson. I wasn't, and never did. The CSE (Certificate of Secondary Education for those of you too young to remember it) was not as good as the GCE (the General Certificate of Education, or the O-level), so I was not allowed to do it. Despite the fact that a grade I in that particular subject was the equivalent of an O-level pass, I was made to take woodwork instead, not by the school but by my mother. Great. Me doing woodwork was like Ozzy Osbourne recording a duet with Julian Clary. I was Julian Clary. Nice subject, but I really was as hopelessly inept as Clary would have been fronting Black Sabbath. And so passed an opportunity to study my obsession from a young age. I failed woodwork miserably. Nobody was particularly surprised, and I got over it without suffering any deep, long-lasting trauma. I did reveal this blemish to Jackson years later while teaching alongside him in the very same classroom in which I would have enjoyed those sports studies lessons – his response was along the lines that he would shake the old girl's hand if he ever met her again.

My earliest years were, therefore, the ones that laid the foundations for what followed. In that sense, I am no different from any other person out there because what we say, do and experience in our formative years does affect what we think and do in later life. A messy parental divorce or three actually affected me very little in the long run, but the minor league results, the Aussie soccer, the Keighley Sunday Alliance and invented football leagues stayed with me, and by the time I left school, without having made the conscious decision to be that way, I was happily ensconced in my own world. I did the things that normal teenagers did – drank cider in the park, had girlfriends (and there were some particularly fine girlfriends), even indulged a little in illegal substances – but there was already more than a small part in me that was different.

Teenagers usually grow out of the latest fad, but there is a part of us that never changes – the things that make you tick in your formative years still make you tick when you move into adolescence, into adulthood and beyond. Beyond my own little world in the 1980s there were facts to be unearthed, details to be discovered and anoraks to be worn.

Chapter Three

BOOKS, BOOKS AND MORE BOOKS

Every good anorak should have in his possession a super selection of books from which a substantial collection of facts and figures can be gleaned. Within these pages should be the answer to everything he may ever need to know. Well nearly. An anorak's other purpose in life is surely to add to the staggeringly huge library of information at his disposal. One should, however, be able to draw upon a number of resources with which to verify one particular statistic. Innocent queries from friends and family members should be diligently researched in order to produce well-informed and precise answers. There should be no confusion as to whether your local football team has won the district cup on five or six occasions, nor whether wartime competitions should be included in this figure or not, or whether the sixteenth incarnation of a once famous club can be construed as a direct descendant of the original or a completely new club. Because you have a huge arsenal of facts, figures and mere trivia with which to fall back on, there should be no disputing your findings.

Furthermore, every book that is in an anorak's collection is catalogued. Not just alphabetically, but by category. After all, why would you place club histories with annuals and yearbooks? Why on earth would you put *A History of Wooldale Wanderers* in the same section as *The Scottish Non-League Review of 1998/99*? Therefore, your rather lengthy list may comprise the following sections for each individual sport: club histories (with separate sections for League, non-League, defunct and overseas clubs), league and cup histories (again, possibly with sub-sections for current and long-gone competitions), regional histories, annuals and yearbooks, statistical books, general reference books, biographies and autobiographies.

There is a reason for this. You really must be able to locate your information in an efficient and timely manner. Plus, by listing them this way it becomes clear that only the 2002 edition of *Tyke Travels* is needed to finish your almost complete list of every Driffield & District Football League final table since 1945. Satisfaction.

Housing your vast library of limited-edition hardbacks, annuals, statistical histories et al is a going concern. The wife is far from happy with this aspect of your marriage. There are moves afoot to convert your loft space in order to add essential shelving to house these publications. And then there is the dilemma of exactly how to store these books in your existing space – bookcase, another bookcase, shelving, floor space, table, windowsill, bureau top, CD rack and fireplace. There needs to be sufficient space for the wife's ornaments, and you don't really want your front room looking too much like a library, otherwise your in-laws will start to talk about you behind your back.

European football yearbooks need to be grouped together, even if they are not all the same size. Your large collection of Scottish amateur football books – all privately published – must not be split up, that would not do. Rothmans and John Player rugby league annuals should really be housed together, despite being entirely separate publications, and obviously the Australian rugby annuals should be in with that lot too. It's not easy. There has to be some order to it all, and it is important to be able to lay your hands on the required information with the minimum of fuss.

A burning issue is what to do with your old annuals, those that are strictly speaking out of date but nevertheless of vital importance should you need to check up on a few facts. There could be no other way to check whether Walton & Hersham FC's secretary did in fact fulfil the same role for Lowestoft Town the previous season. So for this reason they must be close at hand: under the bed, in the spare room or in the loft?

Then there are the obvious subscriptions to consider. Whether it be *The Football Traveller* or the newsletter of the Association of Track Statisticians, it is important that there is at least one periodical any good anorak should look forward to hearing landing on their doormat. There is, of course, usually more than one, as you cannot glean an intensely huge amount of information from merely a single magazine. Other people may be able to, but not the anorak. You may even contribute to one or more of these same publications. It's more of an informal reciprocal agreement really – you digest the information you read and you contribute your information to others who may need or request it, or just have a passing interest in your chosen subject. You receive no payment whatsoever for the information you voluntarily forward to the editor, and you don't really want to be paid. Despite having spent endless hours dissecting, compiling, and finding some order from the pages and pages of facts and figures you have compiled, you are more than happy to offer this to whoever wants it. After all, it cost you nothing more than a small subscription for the stuff you read about in your magazine.

Forget the glossy, colourful periodicals that adorn the shelves of virtually every newsagent in the country, your magazine is available by subscription only, and it doesn't come in a brown paper bag. The only advertisements are for magazines of a similar nature – they all support each other and share a common readership – or for the latest book compiled by a reader. There is no gloss and dross in the world of subscription statto magazines, nothing but statistics, data, league tables and dozens and dozens of obscure results.

Peruse the vast number of available titles out there and you will see what I mean. Standing out among my old man's model railway magazines was the delightfully titled *Philatelic Bulletin*, the doyen of stamp collectors. I kept them safe for him, or so I thought. Among the myriad football publications are lesser known titles such as *The Football Traveller* and *Non-League Retrospect*, their readership of hundreds enjoying what are essentially part-time publications, edited by one or two individuals who have the usual day jobs.

Those with the patience to while away their Sunday mornings on the river bank, meanwhile, might prefer *Fly Fishing and Fly Tying*, which I am assured is packed with features of a piscine nature. You don't have to be a hardened sportsman either. Model engineers can revel in the delights of *Engineering in Miniature*, musicians can subscribe to *Brass Band World*, and there are dozens of birdwatching publications, some glossy on-the-shelves types, others self-produced and aimed at a highly specialised type of twitcher. Travel enthusiasts can choose to purchase *Minor Monthly* (the magazine for the Morris Minor owner and enthusiast) or even *Aeroplane Monthly*, with its details of historical aviation. If only, as a child, I had known about *Short Wave*, then I too could have joined the world of the radio enthusiast. I am currently undecided as to whether I should set up direct debit instructions for *The Erotic Review* or not. I have a feeling that this one deals with a different type of anorak, the very plastic type.

Of course, the average football statistician will have very little interest in most of the aforementioned titles, but they serve the same purpose to thousands – or maybe only hundreds – of equally obsessive individuals around these fair isles.

In the same way that you subscribe to your specialist magazine, there is also your subscription to the latest club history book that has been published. You have your name in the 'advanced subscribers' list at the back. Yours is book number 236, and only 500 were ever printed. You remember the first book you ever subscribed to, and it still sits proudly on your number one bookcase. The football anorak will have a near complete set of *Breedon Complete Histories* and will still be searching for that elusive bargain copy of the Mansfield Town or Bristol Rovers history in order to make that set complete (that's if you didn't write those books in the first place). It may mean a complete set of *Wisden* cricket annuals, where you can almost effortlessly lay your hands on any bowling performance in any Test match since the year dot. You may even be able to describe how UK track and field performances are in decline by referring to the thirty-fourth highest ranking under-17 performance each year in the triple jump. It's important to you, it's useful information for your peers, and you really don't give a damn if it's not everyone else's cup of tea.

Your book, music, programme or cigarette card collection is the tip of the iceberg. You are a forumite. With so much information at your fingertips this is only inevitable. There are a dozen or so internet-based forums to which you regularly contribute. The idea of the online forum is that like-minded people may share information on a related subject and perhaps engage in a little light banter at the same time. You can analyse attendances in each of the step-five pyramid soccer leagues or argue the point that the Eastern Counties League is stronger than the Essex Senior League – and you have the information to prove it. Another forumite can do exactly the same and utterly contradict you. You can share your groundhopping experiences with fellow 'hoppers from around the country. You might even meet up with a few of these fellows when your favourite local team plays a key FA Vase tie in some far-flung backwater.

You may even be able to track down that one person who is willing to sell his Newton Heath FC Baines Shield. Now that would never have been possible before the age of the internet. These were the first ever football and rugby cards, issued in Bradford on thin card from the end of the 1800s. Local schoolchildren collected them and then exchanged them for marvellous gifts that Mr Baines was offering at the time. Many modern-day Baines Shield collectors would accept no gift whatsoever for their prized possessions, even if they do contain the obscurities that were Harewood Hill Side Rovers,

Great Horton Wesleyans and Silverhill Rovers, rather than that much-desired Newton Heath card.

Not everyone appreciates your contribution to the forum. There is little point in being hurt by this. You are, after all, really quite thick skinned. You may be requested to 'go get a life' when you reply to Kev's post on your local Sunday league website. After all, his rather less-than-polite posting about the dire performances recently displayed by Rose & Crown FC's second team was inaccurate. It was their first team who lost by 11 goals on three successive occasions five seasons ago, so this is not their worst run of defeats ever. If only he had done his homework first. And Skinner, who plays at left-back, is not a knobhead.

The crème de la crème of internet forums is that on Tony Kempster's football website. Any self-respecting football geek knows exactly who Tony Kempster is − or rather he will have trawled through his highly informative website a thousand times without actually having met the bloke. Those you come across on Kempster's forum all know their stuff − no insults, personal attacks or naughty words here. If your local semi-professional club goes bust, changes its name or even has plumbing problems in the men's toilets then you will read it here first. If it isn't mentioned then it didn't happen.

A favourite pastime of the anorak is, of course, to peruse the local second-hand bookshop, just as a collector of music will trawl the declining number of second-hand back-street CD and vinyl shops. Here we are dealing with not just any old bookshop, though, as most of them don't really specialise in the kind of books the football statistician, geek or anorak reads. EBay may have the monopoly on rare and out-of-print literature these days – simply because you are likely to be able to pick up a rare copy here for a lower price than at any recognised bookseller – but potentially there are gems to be unearthed in every back-street bookshop in every town, or even in your local charity shop. How many of us have picked up the odd rarity for a knock-down price in Oxfam, Shelter or Age Concern, or even at the local car-boot sale?

When the wife suggests going to the local garden centre a few miles down the road it promises to be a most fruit-ful afternoon. You can drop her off there and visit the local bookseller, which is only five minutes away if you crack on a bit. It doesn't matter whether you visited this particular outlet last week or a year ago, there is the distinct possibility that your most wanted non-League club history is there – a signed one at that. And if it isn't, well, there's always next time. The boss has her plants and ornaments, and you have trawled the shelves of a simply wonderful place and for a few minutes – or even a few hours – have been in a world of your own, not passed by one single publication, oblivious to the world around you, happily perusing away in a way which makes you tremendously content.

Then there are the books that you just wish you could write yourself. You may have contributed to your favourite periodicals, or even contributed a good deal of research to somebody else's pet project, but you really want to produce a comprehensive record of your own work. Would anybody read your work? Would anybody wish to publish it? Does this mean you have to publish it yourself? Exactly how would you put the damn thing together? Who would check your work

– there could be glaring errors or omissions in there that only the most dedicated of your peers would even notice. It's a minefield out there – but you really, really do want to do this. And then you really are on your own. What starts out as an hour every other night quickly becomes an obsession, until your project begins to dominate every moment of your life. You lie awake at night (pen and paper at your side, should there be a 'eureka' moment), mulling over the problems you face. You rise from bed early to structure and restructure your ideas, and you are hooked, completely hooked on what is fast becoming your only raison d'être.

The anorak is also able to spot errors and/or omissions in other peoples' works at once. It really does annoy you when Accrington Stanley are credited with being founder members of the Football League. Accrington FC were founder members of the Football League, in the days when Stanley were not even a sparkle in their founders' eyes. The clubs had nothing in common other than originating from the same northern town. Everyone should know that, shouldn't they? And isn't it annoying when two separate histories of the same club have pages and pages of results that contradict each other, or when different players are credited for scoring the goal that earned them promotion back in 1903. It takes a very special person to be able to spot some of these errors and omissions but someone has to be able to do it, and lets face it, there is at least one slight inaccuracy, misinterpretation or error of judgement – no matter how tiny or inconsequential – in every one of them.

There is one particular type of book that the anorak abhors and that is the trivia book. They are entirely useless. The reason is this: each fact, no matter how inconsequential or seemingly pointless, must have a context. If Wayne Rooney wears size ten shoes then that is fine, as long as this fact is one of a range of interconnected facts – an in-depth study into body-part sizes of English football strikers, for instance. A trivia book will deal with this in isolation, which makes no sense at all to the expert. Unfortunately, grandparents and distant family members are prone to believing that as you are a geek then you would quite happily take possession of such shite on the occasion of your birthday, or even for Christmas. After all, there are lots and lots of things in there that you would surely find fascinating. Wrong. Anything worth knowing in a trivia book is already known to an anorak, and that which isn't did not need to be known in the first place.

Take these two examples:

1. Burton-on-Trent is the only town the length and breadth of England that has had no less than three Football League teams in the past but now has none. And Burton Albion wasn't one of them. The Merseyside town of New Brighton has had two Football League teams in the past. It is not very likely that it will get a third.

2. The Northern League is the second oldest Football League in the world. It was formed in 1889 and Darlington St Augustines were its first champions, beating Newcastle West End on goal difference. West End later merged with East End to form United. Elswick Rangers finished bottom.

Now these interesting little snippets of our history are factually correct. There is no disputing these facts among the learned. However, just as I am unlikely to casually drop them into a conversation with an acquaintance when discussing aspects of the round-ball game, then I would not find them particularly useful unless I were to be reading a history of long-gone football teams, or of lost football clubs that time forgot. Similarly, unless I were taking part in my local pub quiz, I would find the fact that Brann FC were Norwegian League champions in 1963 exceedingly tedious.

Therefore, the *Ultimate World Cup Trivia Book* , for example, is far less ultimate than *The Complete Statistical History of the FIFA World Cup 1930-2006*. Unfortunately, very few family members, particularly one's grandparents, would be inclined to purchase this far more pricey, yet eternally more useful, resource.

On top of this, many of the so-called interesting facts are wrong. An anorak would be able to spot that and the same grandparents would not be happy to discover that the invaluable material they just bought was not of the standard expected by their young upstart of a grandchild. No, this type of book will most definitely not find itself in your library, not even at the back of the loft. More likely it will go walkabout and find its way into one of those charity shops in double-quick time.

Of course, there are genuinely useful books for anoraks on virtually every subject, and you certainly do not have to be a football, rugby or cricket fanatic to appreciate this. Among my particular favourites is *The Origin and Development of Football in Leeds* by Mike Green. It isn't a very large book, but there isn't a wasted space in it, and I am able to glean far more information from one single page in Green's efforts than I am in maybe ten or twenty pages of a glossy mass-market publication based on superstars of the Premiership. Dave Twydell writes volumes – literally – on the likes of *Defunct FC*, *Rejected FC* and *Denied FC: The Football League Election Struggles*, and has reached over thirty volumes of his twice-yearly *Gone, but Not Forgotten* series, which gives broad details on a wide number of obscure teams and grounds that are consigned to our past. You will be hard pressed to find any of these titles on the shelves of WHSmith.

Unless you are a committed Bradford City fan then there are some titles that will just not be on your Christmas list, unless of course football grounds and obscurely titled books are your speciality. Groundhoppers may then appreciate *Putting Valley Parade on the Map: A Short Illustrated History of Valley Parade as the Home of Bradford City and an Impression of that Period*, or even *Along the Midland Road: A History of the Fourth Side at Valley Parade 1886-1997*, both by my friends at the club's very own *City Gent* fanzine. As well written as they are, it would be hard for you to argue that you weren't a little odd should you be found reading one of these in the office or on the bus.

The world of rugby has its fair share of specialist titles too. *Buff Berry and the Mighty Bongers* by journalist Mike Latham takes some beating when it comes to obscurely titled histories. Only a select few outside the north-west of England would ever know who Buff Berry was, and even fewer would know who the Mighty Bongers were.

My current favourite has to be the one that Rupert Sebastian Cavendish put out just prior to the new millennium: *A Guide to the Holding of Sports Books in the Bookshops of Britain*. Please do not try to argue that this isn't aimed at a very specialised audience, and yes, I have used it as a point of reference on more than a handful of occasions. I would commend

Cavendish personally, except that he doesn't really exist. He is the carefully constructed alter-ego of another well-known author mentioned elsewhere in this book. For the record, his choice for 'the number one second-hand bookshop in the whole of the United Kingdom' is the one down the road from my humble abode in sunny Todmorden, right on the Yorkshire/Lancashire border. The proprietor is a cheery chap by the name of Victor Collinge. Now he will have heard of Buff Berry and his Mighty Bongers. In fact, you are just as likely to see him at Cowfoot Lane, the home of the mighty Bacup Borough Football Club of the North West Counties League. You will read more about this lot a little later.

The huge tome of a book that Bill Smith produced in the early 1980s, *Stud Marks on the Summits*, chronicles the history of fell running. It is quite simply the bible of the sport and is so hard to track down these days that those that appear on the best-known online auction sites such as eBay rarely sell for fewer than three figures. I am not saying that everyone who has read a copy of *Stud Marks* is an anorak, but what I am getting at is that among the fell-running fraternity, this tome is the essential item to have.

Anyone who has ever taken part in a long-distance fell race will be all too aware of the one compulsory item you must carry, usually in bum bag: the potentially life-saving anorak. A fully waterproofed, preferably brightly coloured one. Lovely. Yes indeed, some anoraks do wear anoraks themselves – and they usually go on to lead perfectly normal lives. It can be argued that those sports that do not enjoy mass participation, such as fell running, have the most bizarre books ever published, and yet to their readership they are essential.

I know other enthusiasts who have vast collections of match-day football programmes and cigarette cards (of the more recent type than Baines Shields). They face the same problem, namely where to house them all. A complete collection of Coventry City FC programmes will contain all shapes and sizes, ranging from the modern-day gloss and dross to a single sheet of A4, and on top of that almost every opposition team had a programme that was different in shape and size to any other, so if you collect away programmes too you have twice the problem. I shudder to think of the problems that the collector of reserve and youth-team programmes will have in housing these too.

Now there are a number of well-established football programme collectors clubs. They are big business. Contemporary Premiership and Football League issues may be easy enough to get hold of, but those from the 1960s and before that are more highly sought after. You are talking three figures for those from the 1920s – themselves usually no more than single-sheet issues containing team line-ups, a number of advertisements and very little else. Then there are the internationals, the testimonials, the midweek floodlit competitions, the FA Cup League versus non-League specials, and a whole myriad of others. The notion that a match-day programme is valuable only to those who were there at that match is untrue, tens of thousands of collectors will tell you that. The gentleman who recently outbid me for the 1947 York City reserves versus Keighley Town programme on eBay will also tell you that. I bid over £20 for that one.

It should now be obvious that books, and other forms of literature (and this includes anything which is readily available online), are the anorak's best friend. They may represent the foremost indication of your obsessive and maybe compulsive behaviour. What others may see as a bland collection of very boring publications are actually your most consistently reliable and trusted friends.

Chapter Four

STATTO HAS ENTERED THE BUILDING – LIFE AS AN ANORAK

There can't be many of us out there who have not yet come across an anally retentive school or work mate, or wider acquaintance. There are plenty of people that display a tendency to talk bollocks, who insist on telling you what they really want you to know, something which you take not the slightest interest in, and who really do live in a world of their own. They are difficult to ignore, though, and you may be compelled to work alongside them, making life pretty tedious at times.

These very features continued to take shape in my personality as I stumbled through university and moved into the big wide world of full-time employment. I no longer needed to stand behind a rusting set of goalposts on the local recreation ground, or to write poorly constructed reports on my school or village team for the local broadsheet, I had moved on. I may have been at purportedly the least political further education institution in the history of man – you are much more likely to be accosted at Loughborough by a finely tuned athlete wearing a purple tracksuit than by a political activist –

and for a short while my sports reports were replaced by far more mature issues on the editor's letters page in the *Keighley News*.

After all, Thatcher's poll tax *was* undemocratic, and Vince Whitehead was perfectly within his rights to run through the farmer's field that contained the neurotic horse. Heavy stuff for someone who only twelve months earlier did not even know the difference between the Labour, Liberal Democrat and Conservative parties, although it was plainly obvious that I was never going to make it to the House of Commons.

Loughborough certainly offered the life of Reilly for the average, or rather not so average, sportsman. I suspect the fact that I had run for the county schools cross country team had more than a small part to play in my getting on the degree course, even if it was only a BSc (with honours, of course) in sociology. I didn't even apply to get on a sports-related course there, owing to the fact that I was nowhere near international standard at my chosen sport – a pre-requisite for any sportsman trying to get into those areas of study. Contrary to popular opinion, you do need to have some modicum of intelligence to get onto a degree course there – Loughborough students are sometimes unfairly lumped in with the stereotypical Essex girls. Not nice.

The top football team in town, Loughborough Dynamo, was at the time a pretty average parks team, progressing nowhere quickly, yet with no real rivals in the immediate vicinity to worry about (Shepshed isn't far off, but their team were in the Northern Premier League and were therefore light years away in terms of rivalry). I decided to adopt them as my local team, probably because they received quite a bit of attention in the sports pages of the *Loughborough Echo* (which I bought religiously because it contained local football league tables), and although Shepshed received more column inches, their ground was just a little too far away. Besides, I was far too busy following my futile dreams of becoming a world-class athlete to watch local football regularly, although entrance to their Nanpantan Sports ground was free. Good news for any student who has to save his spare pennies as if they were pieces of gold. You had to pay to get in at Shepshed.

Dynamo did not enjoy the best of support anyway. The local leagues in and around Leicestershire are not the biggest of attractions, neither are they enlivened by a bunch of temperamental Italians strutting their stuff on the local playing fields, acting very much like superstars. On occasion, though, I would sit on the fence of the public footpath that ran along one side of the ground before working its way into Charnwood Forest, counting how many times, in a five-minute spell, the word 'referee!' would be used. I still play that game sometimes, and believe me it's much worse nowadays.

I developed a theory at the time that the lower down the league each team was, the more the call for the referee would be heard. This proved to be only partially true, because a team, I found, also made much more use of such calls once they fell a goal behind. Additional to this was the fact that players were also far more keen to get on with playing the game in the first half than following the interval, when many were tired and looking for a quick excuse for their mistimed tackle, dodgy back pass or general inadequacies. In such cases, the term was prefixed by one, several or all of 'foul', 'offside', 'watch the game' or 'what was that?', as well as many far-less-polite terms that I could not possibly tell you here.

On other occasions I would quite literally join one man and his dog at the local playing fields where sides such as Lodge Farm and Shelthorpe played out their North Leicestershire League fixtures. This is the lowest level one can play at in this part of the world but I cared not. I was, more often than not, on my way to the top of some hill and this was an excuse to take in the local scene – for a few moments.

Loughborough's leisure centre was situated right behind Forest Court, my beloved hall of residence for four years. Forest Court was a small, pretty unremarkable place to live if you discount the fact that Princess Diana paid a visit to the leisure centre one day (the reason escapes me), when all the hall cleaning ladies waved their flags and wore their union jack paper hats. I was gutted to discover, years later, that this public building right behind where I lived was built right on the Browns Lane site of the former Loughborough United FC, and this had, in fact, been, in its time, the finest football enclosure the town had ever seen. I was even more devastated to discover later that the small ginnel that ran down the side of the George Inn just half a mile further down the road was the old entrance to the even more ancient enclosure of former Football League team Loughborough FC. How many times had I thrown up down the side of that particular public house, unaware that Arsenal's record defeat had been inflicted only yards away a century earlier?

Ironically, Loughborough Dynamo linked up with the university years later and became a decent non-League team, while a new Loughborough FC has since risen to take on the mantle of challenger to Dynamo's dominance. If only it had happened a few years earlier. On a much happier note, however,

I no longer need to send for copies of the *Loughborough Echo* as the internet allows me to acquire final league tables from this competition with comparative ease.

Subbuteo made a welcome return. It may have been a little past its heyday by then, but I had a younger brother who just had to share in the experience. No shoddy Recticel alternative for him, he had to have the best. So he got it for Christmas one year. My student grant just about stretched to a shiny new set, plus an extra set of Bradford City FC players. What young Manny didn't realise was that by the time he actually received the gift, it was a veteran of all Subbuteo games. It had formed the basis of the 'Forest Court Invitation League' which contained all of three teams. Grillo's Gallopers had been revived, albeit briefly, and they may well have continued as a going concern had I actually had the time to play Manny himself. Alas, I did not have endless holidays, as many believe students enjoy, and I was back at college before I knew it. Gallopers would have to go back into hibernation for the time being.

These were the days before the internet, you have to remember, so Sunday mornings were still pretty darned important. Now that I had a bit of cash I could buy the *Mail on Sunday*, the *Sunday Express*, the *Sunday Times* and, for a preciously short time, the *Sunday Correspondent*. The whole lot. My reason? Well I couldn't miss a non-League football result. I could easily find out how Lodge Farm had fared against Hathern in the North Leicestershire League, but there were the results from up north one had to consider, and remember the Northern Counties East League was brand new. I tried to work out league tables based purely on Saturday afternoon results. I spent hours wondering why reigning champions

Colne Dynamoes had failed to fulfil a single fixture in the new Northern Premier League campaign – it wasn't as easy in those days to discover that this famous little club had dramatically folded during the summer. I was utterly delighted when the first non-League monthly magazine hit the shelves and provided a small number of much-needed answers to my growing list of questions. What did I say about students having to save their pennies? At least this proved to me that I was not the only one with such as obsessive interest. For the first time I could see in the pages of this new magazine that there were others just like me.

The obsession with final league tables continued unabated. Based in another part of the country, a whole range of leagues were introduced, and the local press could always be relied upon to provide the necessary details. There are those who methodically add up each column of each league table they collect in order to check whether said table is actually 100 per cent accurate or not. The odd inaccurate figure bothered me not one jot, as I was, and still am, far more interested in the teams themselves. For the first time, I also began to keep records of local league compositions. In other words, I listed the make-up of each division of each league I could find every season. These are merely lists, and I have now compiled thousands of these. I can tell you exactly how many teams there were in each division in any league, and in any given season. This way I was able to record the demise of the Rotherham & District Saturday League, which in less than a decade went from being a healthy five-division competition to one which was forced to disband through a lack of teams. I could tell you exactly which teams folded during each season, which clubs amalgamated with others and how many times some clubs swapped leagues. Even the Pennine Amateur Rugby League was not exempt from scrutiny.

I also sent a trusty stamped, addressed envelope to the secretaries of many of these leagues. If I was lucky, I would be sent a brand new league handbook. Now how excited do you think I was to receive a lovely little pocket-sized directory containing club details and league tables from a tiny local competition that very few people actually gave two hoots about? You would never get your hands on a Rotherham & District Saturday League handbook these days.

On top of this, my folks sent the *Keighley News* down to Leicestershire every week in order that I could still follow the fortunes of my home town's footballing greats. Juventus may have fallen by the wayside but there were still the likes of Lothersdale Athletic, Timothy Taylors and Market Arms football clubs. Market Arms were a familiar lot – they used to be Mark Burns' Parkwood United. They, too, folded not long after.

Yet I still managed to live a perfectly normal student life. I fitted in as I had done at school. I fell in love, deeply in love, spent a good few months consoling myself afterwards, partied, drank plenty of beer (the phrase 'one pint I'm anybody's, two pints I'm everybody's and three pints I'm nobody's' really did apply), and had time to run for the university in the Birmingham cross-country league and in student events, without quite making it into the first team. I did get to compete at the Don Valley Athletics Stadium in the British Student Games, which were trials for the forthcoming World Games in the same stadium – that was something to be proud of.

Gradually, however, long Sunday training runs began to take on another meaning as I progressed to postgraduate status.

All of a sudden I didn't want to run with the club, the sociable pack run was off the agenda. It's not that I became less sociable, but I decided that I would use this valuable time to kill two birds with one stone. There were non-League football grounds just a little further afield to uncover. The Dovecote was first on the list, but then I could also design a route that took in the grounds of Quorn and Barrow Town, both at the time plying their trade in the Leicestershire Senior League. This was a much higher standard of competition than the North Leicestershire League. With a bit of determination I could find the grounds at Kegworth and East Leake, and even Mountsorrel – no matter that this was usually on a Sunday morning and there was no match being played. I was groundhopping. I never shared this with my flatmates or part-time training partners – I had no need. What possible interest would they find in this? The lads in my flat were, with one exception, among the few Loughborough students who were uninterested in any type of sport other than indoor bowls, and the lads and lasses at the athletic club were too busy becoming international superstars. So while the likes of Tanni Grey and cricketer Nick Knight – both of whom I shared lectures with – were well on their way to becoming sporting stars, I was on my way to becoming a bona fide and genuine football anorak.

There were signs for all to see. Anyone with even half a knowledge of Ordnance Survey maps could quite easily have worked out what I was up to from the myriad multicoloured ink marks drawn onto the ones on my bedroom wall.

Now I know many runners who plot their favourite routes on their wall maps, but how many have every sports ground circled or highlighted at the same time, and how many have those same routes specially planned to take in as many of these grounds as possible?

Armed with a second-class honours degree and newly acquired Post Graduate Certificate of Education (try saying that after a skinful) my first teaching job was a rude awakening to the real world. I had undertaken a teacher-training course as an easy option, an excuse to spend another year being bone idle during the day before committing a little larceny (involving the removal of road or street signs) slightly later on – students will know exactly what I am talking about.

One quickly discovers that a PGCE is anything but easy. Teaching practice in a particularly middle-class middle-England town is not easy, and it is hardly the ideal post for a newly qualified general-subjects teacher back home in 'Rita, Sue and Bob' country. Things got even harder then. I had something to occupy my inquisitive mind other than sport, sport and more sport. I had to do some real work for a change and there was also a mortgage to pay.

Bradford is hardly the most salubrious urban area in Britain, and it may not have the best performing schools, but at least it boasts the headquarters of the West Riding County Amateur Football League. I bought my first house, not more than a mile from the Slack Side Working Men's Club – the official HQ of that very same league. There is a Slack Bottom half a mile up the road.

Within easy range of what was a fairly mundane bachelor pad – complete with centrepiece living-room bookcase filled with football books and tacky athletics trophies – there was a plethora of football grounds, all of which consisted of a railed-off pitch and adjacent clubhouse (manna from heaven for the football anorak). I could cover around four or five of these grounds in one day if I ran hard enough. Saturday afternoon was now long run day (unless I was racing, that is – I still harboured ambitions of becoming much better than I ever would be), and what made these days even better was that at least one of the games would involve the purchase of a match-day programme, something I could never get hold of at Loughborough. Therefore, the first five minutes after 3 o'clock were usually spent watching the early exchanges at Harold Park, then the home base of Wibsey FC (they used to be known as Junction FC you know). I could just about get to sunny Arkwright Street – still home to Tyersal FC – before half-time, or turn south and travel to Brighouse Town. All three clubs produced programmes at the time. I could add these to those I already had for Ventus Yeadon Celtic and VAW Low Moor (please don't ask what the 'VAW' stood for).

Alternatively, there was Campion at the famous old Scotchman Road ground, which even has a stand – a particularly dilapidated one at that, but which has seen many a classic cup-tie over the past half-century. I could go to Fields FC – with their floodlights – at their much more modern Hollingwood Lane base at Lidget Green , or I could even visit Halifax Irish and Ovenden West Riding, who to this day share the same ground high above Halifax. There were others too, and I even wrote about them. Unfortunately, the editor of the *Non-League Traveller* misunderstood my use of the phrase 'running between grounds' and replaced the first word with 'dashing', obviously in reference to a motor that at this time I didn't own. I still hadn't passed my test – maybe I should have clarified that. It was a start, though, and 'Rob Grillo's Travels' made centre pages in two consecutive issues. Now it was official, this was the first time that I had been in print in a national magazine, albeit one with a smallish print run, and I really was an anorak.

It was no coincidence then that I suddenly started to win the odd half-marathon, 10k, and five-mile road race, and I even started to win County Championship medals. Those who said that I didn't do enough quality training just didn't appreciate the effort that went into covering the miles between so many football grounds in a little over an hour and a half. I ran the Bradford Half-Marathon – it started and finished at Thackley FC, and the route passed within yards of the grounds of both Guiseley FC and the uniquely named Crag Road United. I had a quick glimpse of Otley Town's neat little enclosure during the Otley 10 Mile Road Race. If only I had spent a little more time concentrating on the chap in front of me then on each occasion I would have finished first instead of second. The same lad beat me in both races and he went on to run for his country. That was story of my running career – I was never quite good enough.

I also began to frequent the better equipped pyramid grounds of Farsley Celtic and Eccleshill United. There was another reason for this, and it was not for the quality of football that was on offer. At the time, each ground housed a well-stocked club shop. I would often coordinate my arrival with the half-time interval in order to gain free entry, my sole intention to meticulously search through the many programmes, club handbooks, mugs, souvenirs and, most importantly, obscure book titles in order to spend a little more of my hard-earned wage and keep myself happy when it came to bedtime reading. On more than one occasion I left the ground completely unaware of the scoreline – I was not there to see the teams play.

This particular sporting geek had indeed discovered the value of a good book by now. Author and publisher Dave Twydell was partly to blame for that. Once I discovered the array of publications put out by his small company, I never looked back. I already had in my possession all of Tony Williams' *Non-League Directories* up to that point (I was far from unique in this respect because every football anorak has at least a few of these from which to glean vitally important factual and statistical information). I had started collecting these at a young age, and I owned a handful of other run-of-the-mill football books, but once I discovered Twydell's Yore Publications, it was as if the Egyptians had opened the floodgates on the Aswan Dam. An array of football-club histories was further enhanced by a range of books on minor league football, and on long-forgotten clubs and grounds from the distant past. I had dozens of questions waiting to be answered, and suddenly they were there, right in front of me, in print. I finally discovered what had happened to Road Sea FC of Southampton; Bentley Collieries' demise was at last explained to me in glorious detail. I discovered much, much more about the Helensborough and Abercorn football clubs in bonnie Scotland, thanks to the prolific number of self-published works coming from Stewart Davidson north of the border. This was what being an anorak was all about, and it was like opening a box of chocolates, white ones, on a desert island. Except this box of chocolates could be shared with anybody, and once I had discovered my bit of it, I just wanted more and more.

Passing the old driving test is a major watershed in the life of any individual. In my case, it also coincided with the demise of my moderately successful running career, as football grounds from further afield were suddenly thrust into my sights. Here I am not just talking about current enclosures, there were the defunct, built-over, long-gone grounds that I just had to find too. Hence my morning out to sunny Batley. Forget its famous variety club and the array of stars that appeared there, the former home of Brook Sports offered far more to me than Eartha Kitt, Joe Longthorne or Bernie Clifton ever could. The goalposts were still there, while a couple of horses happily munched away, oblivious to the fact that one of the county's top amateur teams had strutted their stuff on that same field over a decade earlier.

Feeling blessed, I drove on the short distance to Huddersfield, where I sought out The Warren – a ground recently vacated by little Bradley Rangers, who had been booted out of the Northern Counties East League. It took a bit of finding but once inside I stopped to consider the situation I had volunteered myself into. There was silence, deathly silence. Not even a solitary bird chirping away in the nearby trees. I was alone, completely isolated from the rest of humanity for just a few moments, yet this is how I wanted it to be. I did not want anyone else there at my side. There was no need for another. I wanted to pursue this quirky obsession of mine alone, without the company of a single soul. And yet I was not alone. Within a few small steps I was back in the real world. I was back in my car and surrounded by humanity again. The occasion represented everything that my fanaticism stood for. There are many fanatics who will have a soulmate, someone with whom to travel to the nearest defunct football ground, by train or by car, a partner with whom to adventure to some far-flung destination in order to obtain a match-day programme. This wasn't me. I enjoyed the conventions, the sharing of experiences in print, but when I was travelling, or researching, or reading, I cared not for a soulmate, I was happy in my own world. If there happened to be others in the vicinity then fine, that did not cause me any problems, and anyone who knows me will testify that I can happily talk all day about my pet subjects. It's just that it is nice to be lost in your own world once in a while.

As my interest in books intensified and my knowledge of the history of sport – football in particular – increased, it was only natural that I should join the club. The club being the recently formed, yet short-lived, Association of Sports Historians (or ASH herewith). Former *Daily Mail* journalist Chris Harte had recently returned from an extended stay in Oz – where he wrote the huge tome that is the *History of Cricket in Australia* – and had been instrumental in the foundation of this rival to the British Society of Sports Historians. This amalgam of like-minded beings was around for less than a decade, moribund only due to Harte's busy schedule after forming the National Sports Reporting Agency, yet it led, indirectly, to the publication of dozens of historical books that otherwise would never have seen the light of day. Rob Grillo has written four of these. I may not have found a subject with which to make a million dollars, but for the first time I had realised that the average working man could also write a book. You didn't need to have a degree in literature or know the right people, you just had to know, or research, an awful lot about your favourite subject. ASH was full of people like myself, we were not merely a diluted group of pseudo-academics, as the well established British Society had become, and Harte himself, who would much rather be seen on the terraces at Halifax Town than Manchester United, encouraged us not to be afraid to come out of the closet. I did and I'm doing just fine thanks.

ASH's annual convention was held all over the place – inside Old Trafford's Salford suite (now we really were treated well that day), and in Glasgow and Worcester, amongst others. It was an opportunity to meet like-minded adults, some of them well known, others barely household names on their own streets, yet all with that common interest in sports history. There were no spotty geeks, even those that delivered a talk on their pet subject were perfectly normal gentlemen (and in one case gentlewoman) leading perfectly normal lives. There was not a hint of pretentiousness, we looked on each other as brothers, we had common experiences, we all knew that Accrington Stanley had never been founder members of the Football League, and for one day a year we ate and drank sport. Harte also produced a quarterly newsletter to keep us up to date with recent events. I looked forward to each issue as much as I did the latest newsletter from Dave Twydell.

The way things were evolving, it was only inevitable that I would embark on the journey to becoming the local sporting anorak. I would write my own book. There was only one thing I could possibly write about, and that was the history of association football in my home town, Keighley – Juventus et al. At least it would sell well there. So I did. As the first through to the eventual fourth books were written, school holidays no longer became a time to unwind, to relax, to do the household chores that I had been putting off for months, they were spent in the local libraries. The lovely ladies in Keighley reference library became my family and could never do enough, they became my closest acquaintances and I still love them a decade later. I trawled the pages of every local newspaper since the year dot, I made lots of mistakes on the way (some of them did not come to light until well after publication), I spoke to local sportsmen (and women), drafted, redrafted (on a school computer as I didn't have my own at the time) and revised. I recapped, rewrote and reorganised along the way until *Chasing Glory* was ready. And not long after that part two, *Glory Denied*, was also ready to be launched to an expectant public.

At last, the Keighley Sunday Alliance could be immortalised in print, the full, unexpurgated history of Juventus FC, of Magnet Joinery FC and of local footballing legends such as the Hockeys, the Hellawells and the Hobsons could be recounted to a readership of hundreds, and the epic encounters at Marley playing fields could be described in their full glory. The long-lost names that had existed a century earlier, such as the oddly titled Victoria Brotherhood, Thwaites White Star and Skipton Niffany Rovers outfits, had been rediscovered at last. I certainly felt as if I had come a long way since my early years hanging around behind the goals at that very sporting venue, maybe a few wish I'd stayed there!

What really amazed me was the sheer number of other souls in the very same reference library. Many were researching their family histories, making use of census data and other computerised records, peering for hours at microfiche documents looking for that one name that would provide the link they have been searching for for months. Others merely browsed the similar rolls of film for reports from the *Keighley News*, or the long-gone *Keighley Herald* and *Correspondent* broadsheets. Others were compiling their own books. I met Don Kirkley, who along with his brother was researching a history of his local rugby club. We both shared the same goal in that we wanted our works to be in print, and in that sense we were both fortunate enough to realise our dreams. It was tragic, then, that Don passed away a matter of months after his efforts finally came to fruition. His brother, David, now also a good friend, continues to write to this day.

Saturday 22 November 1997 should have been a happy, joyous occasion. Instead it was tinged with sadness. The greatest rock star that ever existed was found dead in his Sydney hotel. I was too shocked to appreciate the fact that I was about to strike a book deal, at last, with a Manchester-based publisher. I was far too preoccupied with the untimely and quite tragic demise of Michael Hutchence, whose celebrity I had followed closely since I discovered INXS in the mid-1980s.

Yes, this should have a been a day for celebration, as I had struggled for what seemed an eternity to find anyone interested in publishing my masterpiece. The setbacks I encountered in trying to get the damn things published did little to dampen my enthusiasm. After all, which top author had not had their epic manuscript rejected on more than a handful of occasions before landing that one deal that changed their life forever. I just needed to convince the publishing houses that enough people would buy my work to make it worthwhile. After the arrival of the many expected rejection letters, some of them polite, others far less so, Andy Searle, himself an author, at Manchester's Empire Publications was convinced enough to give it a go. *Chasing Glory* didn't sell that many copies – at least not as many as the follow-up, which Empire also published – but I was in print, I was now an author. However, thoughts of that day when I made the short drive across the Pennines to meet Andy and his boss are tinged with sadness and the memory of a lost soul who had passed away at the other side of the world.

Searle published another book of mine after setting up a new publishing company a few years later, and I even self-published my work on the history of distance running in Keighley – after all, who in their right mind would want to put their money into that, other than a sad geek like myself. Even Andy Searle was wise enough to pass that one up. Remarkably, I was no worse off financially after self-publishing, although the fact that less than 1,000 were produced and that I was well-enough known in the sport to be able to convince enough people to buy it made things a little simpler. (Never proof-read your own work, though – you will know precisely why should you perchance come across a copy of *Staying the Distance*.) These four masterpieces do occasionally pop up on eBay, but don't expect to have to bid too highly for any of them in order to secure your own copy. I have dozens left in my loft.

I now considered myself of the same ilk as the Hartes and Twydells of this world, although I was certainly far less known than either of them. Family, friends and acquaintances, the vast majority of whom had offered nothing but support for my strange behaviour, now had someone of whom they could be proud – and lets face it, with the reputation my family had, they really needed something about which they could be proud. They, and others, could also approach me and say 'you are sad', 'you are an anorak' or 'who on earth would write about that', but I cared not. I could be the most boring fart on earth but I was a member of ASH, I knew Chris Harte and I was a writer. They didn't, and weren't.

Chapter Five

MATCH DAY – THE PEOPLE YOU MEET

In the world of football, an anorak goes public on match day. He meets and greets his audience, his friends and acquaintances who have made that same choice that particular afternoon. These days, match day in the Grillo household involves the ritual that is supporting Silsden Football Club. In the past, and for various reasons, the club of choice has been the likes of Loughborough Dynamo, Bradford City, Wibsey, Farsley Celtic and Keighley Phoenix, but following their remarkable rise through the leagues it is currently Silsden FC. This is my local pyramid club, to whose ground I make the short journey maybe twice a week during the season. After all, I am the authority on local football in these parts, or so I like to think. There is nothing I don't know about the history of soccer in and around Keighley, so it makes sense really that I should follow a local team now that they have taken that big step into the semi-professional game.

Football at this level is the territory of the anorak anyway, so where else would be home from home on a Saturday afternoon, or a damp and soggy Wednesday evening. The solitary anorak is not the only person there, mind you. There may be other anoraks, of course, particularly for those big cup-ties or first games on a new ground.

Silsden Football Club has been around for over 100 years. It was one of the first clubs to be formed in this part of the world, by one of the few better-off Irish immigrants forced by successive potato famines to come here looking for work in the numerous textile mils dotted around the region. Since then the club has dominated the game around here, having won everything several times over. There have been blips along the way: the senior team has folded on more than one occasion, and there was a period in the 1970s when they were thrown out of three leagues in four years due to 'violent and abusive conduct by players and officials both on and off the field', which is about as damning an indictment as you can ever receive. Luckily, things have improved, at least in terms of the behaviour of those running and playing for the club.

The current side reformed towards the end of the nineties in what is essentially the second lowest league to which they could have been allocated to – the second division of the Craven & District League. This league caters for village sides around the Keighley and Skipton region and here is the world of the farmer's field that doubles as a part-time football pitch – the removal of sheep poo is often the first task to be undertaken on match day, either that or the rounding up of horses from the field of play. Silsden could have been placed even lower – this former youth team, who only wanted to stick together for a bit longer, could have placed in the league's third division, at the very bottom. Luckily, the Craven League committee must have had an inkling that they were destined for great things – they weren't wrong.

Less than a decade later, and with countless promotions, cup-final victories and league championships under their belt, the same side (with a few subsequent experienced additions) are in the top division of the North West Counties League, only one step below the Northern Premier League. Heady heights indeed, and unprecedented in this part of the world. The club has progressed to such an extent that their home ground just outside the village does not meet league requirements, necessitating a move down the road for the first team, to Cougar Park, the home of Keighley Cougars Rugby League Club, where ground rent and other charges mean that they now make no money at all. Still, without their hosts, the club would never have been able to make that move up and it's a pity no other team from Keighley has ever made use of the facilities here. But enough of that – here we are with Silsden FC instead, one hundred years ago taking on the might of Thwaites White Star and Skipton Niffany Rovers at grass-roots level, now vying for supremacy among the likes of Salford City and FC United of Manchester.

In terms of following your local team, at this level you are not an anonymous face in the crowd, you are an individual. One half of those there are friends or acquaintances of yours, and there is a fair chance that those who are not are still known to you anyway, at least by sight. The individuals who frequent Cougar Park for their North West Counties League fare could be at any ground at this level in the country, so why not meet some of them. Their names may be different from many of those that you know at your local club, but their traits and aspirations are not. They recognise each other on the terraces week in, week out.

They recognise each other when they meet in the local super-market or garage forecourt, and they know instantly that they share the same goals on a Saturday afternoon. They share these goals and frustrations with their team just as the tens of thousands at Old Trafford, Anfield and Stamford Bridge do, and they are every bit as committed to their club as anyone in the Premiership and Football League.

This is not to say that there isn't the occasional oddball present, the type who nobody else in the ground knows. Not that long ago a rather strange gentleman asked me who the team in red warming up was, prior to a midweek home game. 'Silsden,' I replied, to which the response was, 'Oh, never heard of them.' Odd. The only conclusion I could draw from this was not that he was a groundhopper – sorry, football traveller – who had got himself a little confused and ended up here instead of Colne, or maybe Nelson up the road, but that this gentleman had obviously not paid his fiver to get in and must surely have just awoken from the an almighty slumber fol-lowing an alcoholic binge after the last rugby match to have been played at the ground, and that must have been some four months earlier. Either that or he had delivered his ageing grandmother to the bingo competition in another part of the ground and had wandered into the main stand merely to pass the time. I never saw him again.

The groundhoppers that you do meet at this particular ground could well be at odds with one another. Should they have made that short detour to Keighley Road, Silsden's spir-itual home, en route? There are some that will indeed have made that brief journey, others only if there was a sched-uled competitive fixture going on there. Either way, you can guarantee that they will have discussed this matter at least before the referee has sounded his final whistle at the current home of Silsden's first team.

You could argue that the officials at clubs such as Silsden are more committed to their cause than those in the higher echelons of the game, because at this level they do it for free. Each and every one of the club secretaries, programme editors and committee men are in full-time employment elsewhere. They all have to get up and go to work before spending their evenings and most of their weekends – their precious spare time – organising coaches to away games, running raffles to raise money for the forthcoming season, visiting the launderette, paying affiliation fees and the like. Silsden are not alone in having their share of dedicated enthusiasts running the club, just as they are not alone in playing host to the anorak – and some of these club officials are happy to admit that they themselves double up as anoraks.

Why anoraks? Why not? They possess as much dedication as any statistician in getting things right, arranging, rearranging, revising and reviewing, and they certainly receive very little, if anything at all, for their efforts – save the satisfaction of another Saturday afternoon league victory. Their main dinner-party topic may well be the events of the previous afternoon – the sendings-off, the lack of discipline shown by their star player, or another poor attendance which is severely affecting club finances.

If they are anoraks, then surely the fans are too. Never mind the wives and families of those on the field, think of the dedicated few who turn up at the same turnstile week in, week out for their weekly fix. You have to be pretty committed to follow a club most have never heard of, never mind paying out your well-earned wage to watch on a weekly basis. There is comradeship in this, and lets face it, you are a lucky man if there are any associates at work with whom you can discuss the Silsden versus Colne local derby, and there will be fewer who will have witnessed the amazing comeback by the home team, the debatable penalty, and the blatant offside that the liner missed.

Among those others who frequent this particular sporting arena alongside the 'Lost in Barrow' Robinson clan and I are a number of hardy individuals. They are all unique and as dedicated to the side as anyone at your local non-League club, and they are all part of the anorak family.

One of the first you will come across once inside the ground is committee member Jim Rosser. In fact, you will hear him first. That's because he always has the microphone in his hand. A retired geography master (all the best people are or have been geography teachers), Rosser, whose claim to fame is having groundhopped in Finland, is not to be taken lightly. He may not look particularly scary, but he does not mince his words, and with the whole park in your range, you can say exactly what you want to say – well, within reason anyway. League of Wales club Porthmadog recently earned themselves a three-point deduction and a hefty fine following an outburst by one of their officials.

Rosser, in his role as coordinator of the tannoy system, feels it necessary to have his sole ABBA CD blasting out before each and every home fixture. Now I don't mind listening to 'Dancing Queen', but I'm not totally convinced that this is the tune the players should be emerging from the tunnel to week in, week out. There again, neither is 'Gimme, Gimme, Gimme (A Man After Midnight)'. Jim Rosser is a particularly funny man, though. His particular strength is his ability to produce sidesplitting one-liners during breaks in play – and there have been quite a few of those. During one ugly incident a couple of seasons back – resulting in all twenty-two players conversing in a less-than-gentlemanly way in the centre circle – Jim seized the opportunity to say: 'While we enjoy this short break in play I would just like to declare that today's attendance is 124. I hope you are all enjoying the quality of football on offer this afternoon.' The referee, who was having an off day, failed to appreciate the humour and promptly sent a player from each side for an early bath. Rosser went unpunished.

When questioned, Rosser protests:

> I am not a football anorak. That's because I have a life outside this football club. But I am an anorak when it comes to researching my family history. Did you know that I have traced my lineage back to the 1500s? Which brings me onto some strange tales that I must tell you about my ancestors…

At this point I usually make my excuses and move on.

One must remember, however, never to criticise the Silsden FC club captain while in earshot of Mr Rosser because young Michael Rosser just happens to be Jim's son – and if Jim doesn't hear you, his wife Margaret will. She may be one of the smallest people in the ground, but to make up for her lack of height she is blessed with the most audible voice. She never misses a home game, unless of course she is groundhopping in Finland. Even Michael Rosser has no choice but to listen to his mum.

'My Jim is no anorak,' she protests, hoarse from her latest protestations with the match-day officials. 'At least until he traces his family history. Did you know that he has traced it all the way back to the 1500s?' I move swiftly on again. Ironically, Margaret is also a retired geography teacher. What is it with geography teachers and obsessive behaviour?

Just as the Rossers are household names in this part of the world, so are the McNultys. Chelsea have Roman Abramovich, Silsden have Sean McNulty. One is a famous Russian multimillionaire, the other a groundsman and gardener for Bradford Metropolitan Council. One throws millions of pounds at his latest toy, while the other earns a meagre wage, almost every spare penny of which goes into his village side. Yet the two have much in common: both have an overriding love for their club, they live and breathe football and their dedication (or is it obsession?) is unquestioned. McNulty was a promising goalkeeper, once on the books of Wolverhampton Wanderers, but failed to make that final step into first-team football before the club went bust and were forced to release him. A car accident prematurely brought his career to an end but, like many others before him, he did not lose his love for the game and wanted to put as much back in as he had taken during his playing career.

Silsden's chairman may not have millions, but he is considered to be worth his weight in gold in this part of Yorkshire, and he has got one up on Abramovich – his rising star of a son Danny is now a regular at right-back for the Cobbydalers first team. This, he tells me, makes him 'very nervous on match days'. In addition, Sean's old man is a lifelong Silsden stalwart and – surprise, surprise – his younger brother Jason is manager of the club's highly successful Sunday team, who have probably won more trophies in the last couple of years than their Saturday counterparts. No wonder he is nicknamed the 'Sunday God' in this part of the world. There are countless other sides operating under the Silsden banner too: reserve, academy, ladies, and a myriad of junior teams – the McNultys are involved here too, as well as a large number of other utterly dedicated mums, dads, coaches, and the like.

Jason McNulty's missus, Michelle, is also a regular at Cougar Park, and even more regular on the club website forum, which can be pretty manic at certain times of the season. A typical day will see the likes of 'Gazzer', 'Kingy', 'The Spanish Omelette' and 'Young Gun no. 2' discussing (or inventing) the latest club news, and not without a fair bit of humour along the way. Much of it has been aimed at Martin Bland recently, due entirely to the fact that, despite being one of the club's best-loved sons, he is the biggest wind-up merchant this side of Watford gap. Blandy is no prima donna, though, and is happy to receive his fair share of good-natured abuse after he has posed as a high-ranking club official on the forum and declared that the following weekend's fixture has been cancelled due to an outbreak of anthrax in the club changing room.

There are very few dickheads around on the Silsden forum – they prefer to frequent the more local league and club forums that are knocking around, many of which have subsequently been forced to close down as a result of antics that usually border on the malicious and slanderous. No chance of any of this on the Silsden forum as it is mostly good-humoured banter between players, officials, supporters, opposing teams and, of course, local anoraks, save for the odd mischievous miscreant who is quickly outed.

Next there is Pete Hanson, a man who enjoys posting on the forum so much that he has a multitude of aliases. He also edits the club match-day programme, so he can quite easily claim to be something of an anorak. Producing something of this kind is not as easy as it may sound. How many of us prefer the more mundane aspects of the job such as stapling pages together, visiting the printers once or twice a week, chasing club sponsors up for adverts, or even missing the first twenty minutes of each game to take the money from the punters at the turnstile (did I mention that he also fulfils that role too)? Hanson enjoys his role and has even been known to pour the half-time cups of tea for visiting officials. More on that task later.

Once in his rightful place in the stand, there is only Jim Rosser who can claim to have more of a vocal presence than Hanson, and he has the advantage of having a microphone. 'I hope Pete hasn't seen that,' cries Rosser as the referee makes yet another odd decision. If he has, then the referee is going to have to endure a long afternoon and Silsden are one step closer to losing three points at the next league meeting.

John Barclay is the senior secretary at Silsden FC. He too has caught the bug. Cajoled into a place on the committee by former manager Andy Geary three or four years back, he has become one of Silsden's foremost officials. Over the past twelve months he has been the forum's most regular poster, 'in order to let the people know what is going on at the club,' he adds. Of course, we all believe him. Barclay assures me that he is also actively pursuing a possible sponsorship package with a local company (as yet un-named, but nonetheless one to which clubs like Silsden owe their very existence). The Silsden FC raffle is JB's forte, though, not that he organises the thing, but he usually wins the bottle of scotch that has been kindly donated by one of his fellow officials. Barclay deals with the club paperwork, and let's face it, you have to be pretty dedicated to voluntarily take on this task, unless you are an anorak at heart and revel in the multitude of official statistics and records that must be diligently collated and reported. What a good chap he is.

You could argue that Barclay and Hanson are anoraks. They could be at home in front of a TV on a damp Wednesday evening in February, they need not trail out in the wind and rain just because they are committeemen, but they do, because Silsden is their life and soul. Silsden, and other smaller clubs, bring together people from all walks of life towards a common cause, one which most other people around town don't give two hoots about. Furthermore, ask them if they actually consider themselves anoraks and you will not be disappointed (and they will not try telling you about their family tree – even if they can follow their blood lines all the way back to 1500). If gents like this weren't around, then neither would our local football clubs be.

Further proof that Hanson and Barclay are fully-fledged anoraks is that they are among the few who will not just be spotted at first-team fixtures. They will be there when Silsden's successful academy team are at home – they too have been forced through league rules to play at Cougar Park – and they will be at Keighley Road to see the reserves. They will also follow the reserves and the academy team away from home if there is no first-team fixture. They are supporting their club; nobody is forcing them to go, there are no rules that say club officials have to be there, but they choose to go for one reason, because that's where Silsden Football Club have a fixture. And so they have to be there too.

It will not surprise you that Pete Hanson's two lads have also recently donned the red jerseys of Silsden FC, and that John's little 'un is a regular in the kiddies' teams, alongside a little lad who goes by the name of Geary. Talk about keeping it in the family – would you get that at Stamford Bridge?

Geary is another famous name in this part of the world, again for all the right reasons. Andy Geary was one of Keighley's ace goalscorers in the 1980s. He played for all the top local teams, scored regularly against Silsden for the old Keighley Town FC (don't get me started on that one, I could write a book about Keighley Town. Hold on, I did write a book about Keighley Town didn't I?), and is still heavily involved in the game. He is without doubt the most successful manager in the history of association football, having guided the Silsden first team to what seems like thousands of promotions in barely a decade, and a whole host of cup-final victories. He then stepped down and handed the role to his assistant, Paul Schofield.

So what does Andy Geary now do in his spare time when he is not hauling his ladder up the side of your house to clean your windows? Why, he is coaching Silsden's under-12s team, the very side that his young lad plays for. He is at every committee meeting, watches the reserves regularly, and has even been known to fetch the cups for the half-time tea at home fixtures. Dedication or obsession? Putting something back into the club or an anorak? He did come to one of my talks at Keighley library a few years back – he made up one third of the audience, one of the other two being the librarian – so he must be an anorak because everyone around here knows that my public appearances are pretty drab occasions, and he did say he enjoyed it. Honest.

The club physio, Michelle Brook, is getting pretty famous these days. She soon found herself the star attraction on YouTube when she was forced into action in front of over 3,000 fans at the FC United away game at Bury late in 2006 to attend to a prostrate player. What better stage than this to get noticed? This is the well-publicised breakaway Manchester United supporters club, formed by disenchanted anti-Glazer fans. The FC United lot wanted to sign her up, and they sang about it while she worked wonders on her injured patient. You can understand why they sang about her, those golden locks and that athletic presence are enough to momentarily stop more than a few hearts while she is attending to what seem to be a suspiciously high number of groin injuries sustained by Silsden FC players.

You do not have to be an anorak to appreciate this point, or the next, as no male supporter will deny that they are just a little bit pleased when up-and-coming midfield maestro Sam Dowgill is playing. This is quite simply because if Sam is strutting his stuff for the club, then that means his mother will be there. And if Julie Dowgill, the 'English Rose', is there then we have yet another distraction, the type that often causes us to miss that vital, split-second, match-winning moment at the other end of the pitch.

Julie is actually the only person I have ever worked with who will happily discuss the everyday events at Silsden Football

Club at any time of the day, and who is able to provide me with the latest gossip on transfers and general shenanigans down there. At least she tells me she doesn't mind.

Away fans are not always in abundance at this level of the game, but there is usually a fair sprinkling of them about on match day. They may have travelled the 100-odd miles up from Stoke-on-Trent, and may not be family members or have a position on the visiting clubs' committee. They are following a team that most people from their own town have probably never heard of, never mind support. So what does this say about these individuals? They must be obsessive. After all, what glory could they possibly gain from following Stone Dominoes, or Eccleshall or Newcastle Town all the way up to this particular part of West Yorkshire?

You see these people at your ground season after season, and you remember their cheery faces each time. They request a match-day programme via snail mail should Pete Hanson sell out of them on the day, and they always give thanks for the hospitality at half-time – especially when it is freezing, and your warm drink in the comfort of a room glowing with like-minded souls lifts them to greater vocal highs during the second half. They may not be happy once the final whistle has sounded, though, when they face the long trek back home safe in the knowledge that their side has turned in an abject display for the fourth week in succession, and face almost certain relegation at the end of what has been a particularly demanding campaign.

Yes, of course you have to be an anorak to travel all that way for a team, or a match that ninety-nine per cent of all football fans do not even know is taking place. The Silsden lot know exactly what it is like, the very individuals in this chapter can be seen making these same journeys for Silsden's away games, and they too are treated with the polite respect that is always missing from the upper echelons of our beautiful game. Welcome to the world of non-League football.

At least if you do make that long journey to see the game you should have very little problem parking (assuming you have managed to locate the ground without any problems). There are no special match-day car parks charging a fiver to place your closely watched vehicle on the local school playing fields, you can park up at five to three and still make it with a couple of minutes to spare at most North West Counties League grounds on a Saturday afternoon.

Tim Lees doesn't have to make too far a journey to Keighley. His team, Atherton Laburnum Rovers, are one of two teams in the league from this small town adjacent to Bolton. He has won awards for being an anorak. He produces his club's match-day programme – except in this case the 'match day' part of the title is something of a misnomer. The *Crilly Park Review*, as it is called, requires much more than ninety minutes' reading. It is a monster of a production, yet still only costs a pound. Forget the gloss and dross that costs three times that much in the Premier League – you can read those things in about ten minutes – the programme that Lees produces for crowds that are lucky to break into three figures are like nothing I have ever seen before. I defy anyone to read a copy inside a couple of hours, and what's more, it is entirely readable. Of course, there are the usual adverts that are the life blood of clubs like this but in seventy-odd pages there is no end of material to peruse at your leisure.

You expect the usual team line ups, the managers and editorial pages and a little bit of club history – standard fare at this level – but what comes next is a real labour of love. The following pages comprise this: two pages of match reports, two pages of NWC League tables, eight pages containing results, fixtures and attendances from the same league, two pages on results from the league cup competitions, a page detailing club websites, three pages dedicated to the Atherton LR youth teams, two extra news pages, a page on the reserve team, eight pages of official NWC League news, a player profile page, six pages containing the season's statistics so far, four puzzle and joke pages, five pages dedicated to their opponents – in this case Silsden FC – a 'looking back' page, and then a whole host of pages detailing up-to-date results and tables from the northern pyramid and North West Counties League feeders, or, to be precise, three for the Conference Leagues, six for the Northern Premier League, and then two pages each for the Northern Counties East, Northern, West Lancashire, Lancashire Amateur and Manchester Leagues.

I have paid a tenner or more for books that contain less information than this, and remember that this particular fellow is not getting paid a penny for his efforts. Exactly how Tim Lees, as well as Pete Hanson, finds the time to put this kind of thing together every other week, and sometimes twice a week if there are midweek fixtures, is beyond me. He does not even remotely resemble Roy Cropper, and has no problems or hang-ups when it comes to communicating with others. He has the patience to sit and discuss the world of non-League football with me a couple of times a year so he must be pretty normal. What he does is over and above the call of duty, but he enjoys what he does, and those who read his match-day programmes are eternally grateful for all his efforts – even if there are not an awful lot of us who watch Atherton Laburnum Rovers too often.

Tim himself is uncertain about the future of his favourite pet:

> I've struggled with it recently with not being so well, even thought of packing it in, but I expect I'll do at least one more season after this. Strange how certain hobbies and interests get sneered at. There are some that I don't understand the pleasure of, but if it makes the person happy then so what?

I couldn't agree more. I hope he continues to produce the programme for many years to come, and it is nice to see that he has been recognised by the League and 'programme clubs' because he has won awards for his *Crilly Park Review*. Go out and buy one now. Oh, and if you're still not impressed with that, then check out the club website – Tim Lees is the master of that too.

In typical anorak style, Lees and I usually discuss pyramid matters while our respective teams battle it out on the pitch. While Silsden puff and pant to a nerve-jangling 4-3 league cup victory in bitterly cold surroundings, we reflect on the benefits of the whole pyramid system itself.

'Twenty years ago we were in the Bolton Combination, which was then six steps from the Football League,' my acquaintance muses. 'Since then we've spend hundreds of thousands on ground improvements, gone semi-pro, and been promoted several times and where are we now? Six steps from the Football League. Is it all worth it, I ask myself?'

I can tell you there are thousands of others who would have plenty to say about that. Every single one of them well versed on the subject of the FA's grass-roots revolution that has taken place over the past few years. We no longer have a haphazard system of competitions beneath the top levels of the game; we now have a haphazardly organised system in its place.

There are a myriad of other people you are guaranteed to meet at Silsden Football Club who are deserving of a mention, as there are at any club of Silsden's standing. I know that Silsden don't exactly attract huge numbers of followers, but I could write a chapter about each and every one of those who do follow – even that proverbial one man and his dog. It is easy to wax lyrical about fellow author Ronnie Wharton, who can fit in over 300 games a season, most of them with his equally prolific son, Ian (whose more-than-patient wife will no doubt suffer the same despair as my own). Whether it be a North West Counties League fixture, a local Sunday cup final or a Doncaster Senior League title decider, they will be there. And they do not stand out in the ground as sad anoraks, they are a couple of particularly pleasant chaps who are just as comfortable discussing the subject of many of Ronnie's other publications – boxing – as they are a game of football.

There is also Roger 'the Dodger' Ingham. This unique individual is vice-president of Silsden Football Club and was Yorkshire TV's sporting hero of the year in 2005, due to his dedication to coaching youngsters in virtually every pastime that has ever been invented. Even the Queen appreciates Roger's contribution to the world of the sport as she gave him an MBE early in 2007. As a result, he is now able to herd his cows through the centre of London without fear of enduring the wrath of the local constabulary. Anyone who knows Ingham well enough will know that one day he is likely to do just that.

In this part of the world Roger has been quite rightly labelled 'Mr Sport'. There is not a soul involved in any sport in the Craven district of North Yorkshire that he does not know or has not heard of. And he will have known their fathers and grandfathers too. He is employed as public announcer at an array of Yorkshire Dales sporting events and will divulge at length the full athletic careers of each and every competitor in the fell race. He will also be able to recite from memory every winner of the Kilnsey Sports handicap mile since the war, and as the open-mile winner approaches the final bend and launches himself down the home straight, Ingham will recount that same race some two decades earlier when said athlete's late father won in identical circumstances. He will not pause for breath, he will talk relentlessly, and not one person within earshot will be in any doubt as to who is the most knowledgeable yet highly entertaining man at that venue. Ingham is a natural showman, but by heck does he know his stuff. Sit alongside him at Cougar Park and you can forget about the match you paid to watch, Ingham is just as entertaining.

I could also tell you lots about ever-popular match-day coor-dinator Dave Maxted, who never stops grinning like a Cheshire cat; the hard-working stewards, such as Richard Brook and Gary Creighton, who have been known to remove their bright yellow stewards' jackets in order to berate opposing players and match officials; and the many junior supporters who are among the most vocal set of fans I have ever met. But there is just one other person who I have to share with you. He is without doubt the biggest anorak at this particular sports club, if not in the whole of Keighley, and he is immensely popular for it.

By day he is a super-head at one of inner Bradford's most challenging secondary schools. By night he attends the regular meetings, parents evenings and other hugely important occasions that every good professional must make part of his daily itinerary. He stays right until the end too. At weekends he is transformed (he is also transformed on a Wednesday evening during the football season, or even on a Tuesday evening, events permitting, if the club are playing away, and even on a Thursday evening if Silsden are away at Bacup Borough), leaving home at all times with his trusty camera and its attendant tripod.

There are some things of which we can be 100 per cent sure. We know the sun will rise every morning, that Christmas day will be on 25 December each year, that every fourth year will be a leap year and we know, we just know, that Mr David Brett will be behind the opposition goal on match day. And he will not miss that defining moment in the game, even if Julie Dowgill is in the main stand – the shot that will appear in the *Keighley News* on Thursday morning. You know very well that he will be at your local village fête alongside the winner of the largest radish competition, and at that six-mile fell race across the Brontë Moors. He will be there at the start, at the halfway point and, somehow, poised with camera at the finish. He has still not yet managed to explain to me how he achieves this feat.

This particular enthusiast even runs the Silsden Football Club website as well as his own, which catalogues the many snaps he has taken, and he moderates the club forum. The two words 'Where's Bretty?' comprise the most commonly used phrase in the main stand at this club. He may be late at times (the prize giving at Keighley agricultural show may have overrun or there may be controversy regarding the authenticity of that radish), he may even be stuck in traffic, or lost, if Ian Robinson has given him directions, but David Brett will be there, and so will his camera. 'I just enjoy what I do,' he claims. What he probably hasn't fully grasped yet is that others enjoy what David Brett does just as much as he does.

David Brett would happily take his place on the Silsden Football Club committee, but I think you will understand why he claims not to have the time. Somehow he has a hobby too, a different one. You would never realise from meeting this rather mild-mannered gentleman that he was also a rather well-respected thespian with the local amateur dramatic society. I have been reliably informed that he has recently made the role of Friar Tuck his own, and I have every reason to suspect that beneath his regulation brown habit is a smart new bright yellow anorak.

If you happen to wander down to see Silsden FC one day you will actually see these people. They really do exist. They are not nameless faces in the crowd, they are individuals. They matter, they make a difference and they are utterly dedicated, or is that addicted, to Silsden FC. They are also lovely people. Not one of them can ever be accused of being sad, because they aren't sad, but they are anoraks all right. Each and every one of them possesses immaculate social skills and they all lead fulfilling social lives. They are articulate, and are more than happy to engage in conversation on a topic other than their local football club.

You will not find them huddled together in an exclusive part of the ground. Although many of them prefer the comforts of the not particularly state-of-the-art main stand, you could wander around to the shed end of the ground behind one the goals and find a fair sprinkling of these hardy souls there. David Brett will wave if asked. There are people like this down at your local club too, alongside the occasional groundhopper. You could quite easily be one of them.

Chapter Six

MY FAMILY AND OTHER VICTIMS

It is impossible to lay the blame for my unhealthy obsession with any member of my family. My folks split up when I was relatively young, my old man has spent many of the subsequent years in her majesty's pleasure, and the stepfathers that followed were not around long enough to cause any lasting damage. So I can only blame myself – I understand people are prone to do that.

There was a particular bonus involved in going to Whitakers newsagents shop at Stockbridge all those years ago, and that was Louise Preston. Her parents owned the shop and she was lovely. Her long, straight, brown hair and blue eyes stole my heart for what seemed an eternity, but was probably only a few weeks – still a fairly long time for a young lad not even close to his teenage years. Checking out the previous afternoon's football results was one thing, but Louise Preston made that ten-minute walk, in wind and rain particularly, very worthwhile. An anorak in the making I may have been, but my unhealthy obsession with the irrelevant did not preclude any interest in the opposite sex.

I have no idea what became of Louise Preston, she probably married a man with far more interesting things to do in his spare time, but many years and several close shaves later there is a lady lucky enough to be called Mrs Grillo. She is revered among her peers for her patience and fortitude – after all it is not easy living with the most boring man on earth, and there have been plenty of occasions when one's status of anorak does not fit comfortably with that of devoted husband.

The wedding day was fraught. Wedding days are usually quite fraught – most married people can tell you that – but in my case it wasn't that things were going belly up. Both bride and groom had turned up, the rings were safely where they should have been and there were no last-minute revelations that could have blown the whole thing to pieces. It was fraught because I was missing what was potentially the match of the season.

Bradford City, hoping at the time to return to the Premiership as soon as possible, had a key League fixture at home to local rivals Burnley. It was a game I would not normally have missed. Non-League grounds had temporarily been consigned to a once-fortnightly role as my childhood heroes, Paul Jewell's 'Bradford Army', took their unlikely place in the FA Premier League, and then dropped down back again. I had splashed out and purchased a season ticket in their first Premier League season and for a couple more years renewed it at the season's end. This was City's first season back in the second tier and an early return to the top flight was seen as entirely achievable, but that season ticket was useless on this particular day.

I had been warned that any attempts by the guests to keep me informed of the score, no matter how important the fixture was, would be met with reprisals. She may be small, but Mrs G is not to be taken lightly, particularly on her wedding day. We were on a gorgeous Scottish isle surrounded by an elite gathering of family and friends. The sun was out (yes, it does occasionally reveal itself in this part of the world), we were based in the gardens of a beautiful country hotel – the quaintly named Auchrannie – and there was much to be jovial about, even if the piper had to cancel at the last minute. After all, it's not every day you get married (unless you are my parents, of course, who have been wed no less than seven times, at the last count, between them).

By the time Sue and I had exchanged vows, City were trailing 1-2. As we cut the cake they were down to nine men – two sent off in controversial circumstances – and as we got stuck into our first course at the wedding breakfast the game was deep into injury time. Sixteen of the seventeen persons present were well aware of this, including the chief bridesmaid, and only one person was blissfully unaware of the dramatic events that were unfolding back down in not-so-sunny Yorkshire. City's last-gasp equaliser was the most talked about goal that season, and a couple of hundred miles up the road, across the Firth of Clyde, almost every single individual at that wedding had heard the news within seconds.

It was some months before the seventeenth person discovered the truth behind the events of that day. My testicles still bear the scars to this day, but I must add that thanks to my good self a not dissimilar situation arose during my brother's wedding some two weeks later. Alas, the score on this occasion was a dull, lifeless, goalless draw and Manny's nether regions remained unscarred.

Circumstances dictated that our honeymoon should actually be prior to the wedding itself. The then future Mrs G had every opportunity to change her mind. She bit her lip as we flew over Newfoundland, and I chattered away to all and sundry about the tombolos, barrier beaches and spits I could clearly make out below. I just thought that people would want to know, having being newly installed as head of geography back at Greenhead and all that. On a gorgeous Nova Scotia beach I marvelled at the array of stacks, stumps, arches and wave cut platforms on the beach. The rest of our whale-watching party became quite quickly bored with my enthusiasm for such landmarks, and Mrs G wondered why I had to be standing so far away as I photographed her on the golden sands. Did she know that in order to get an entire arch into shot you have to be some distance away?

It was Sue who first coined the term 'anoraknophobia' in our household. She is afraid of spiders, and I mean really afraid, but she seems far more prone to suffering the intensely stolid and cheerless role of wife of anorak than she does victim of an eight-legged arachnid. And there are the phone calls she is forced to endure. 'Rob, there's another anorak on the phone,' is quite possibly the most overused phrase in our part of Yorkshire these days.

It is appropriate then that an author of several highly specialised local sports books should answer queries and take orders for his publications over the telephone. It is merely part of the service. Some of those good enough to part with their money may wish to talk for a short while, I may even wish to talk for a short while – I'm good at that. This may mean that *Coronation Street* or *Eastenders* must be reduced to backing-track status while a frank discussion on the merits of the creation of a sixth step-five league in the non-League pyramid takes shape. Not everyone is happy with this arrangement. We have Sky Plus now, so that problem has gone away, hasn't it?

On our fourth wedding anniversary we received the usual congratulations cards from family and friends, although one was a little different. The best man, littlest brother Manny, bought Mrs G a sympathy card. Of course it was a joke but it summed her situation up perfectly. It can never be easy living with an anally retentive husband, who offers more than a hint of a highly obsessive personality. But there again, my dearly beloved did know what she was letting herself in for, all the signs were there during our courtship, it's just that once the honeymoon period is over you start to pay more attention to the things that have always slightly irritated you. I have always loved cheesy, camp eighties music – I certainly did when I met the future Mrs G on our blind date that went a little too far. I made no attempt to hide my collection of euro-disco CD singles and albums during our early months together, played them at an unacceptably elevated volume in my decaying Ford Fiesta as we stepped out together, while my Saturday afternoon ritual at local soccer matches was never in danger of being checked.

Marriage failed to dampen an enthusiasm for things that I should have grown out of years earlier. There are some things in life, a wedding for example, that take precedence over everything else. Your marriage is the most sacred and devout undertaking to which you will commit yourself, yet there is still some desire to hold on to that immensely gratifying hobby or interest that you are not particularly interested in sharing with the wider world, let alone your loved one.

There is a routine to which Mrs G is now dearly accustomed: the words 'Back just after five' on a Saturday about half past two, at least for Silsden FC's home fixtures (it can be much later than that if the game is away from home); the cluttered mess on the mantelpiece where today's mail, packets and parcels lie, placed there for me to peruse at my leisure when I return from work; the small diversions undertaken when driving through an unfamiliar town or village, in order to 'just see where the local football team play'; and the countless tacky and rather grubby back-street shops that really don't need to be searched from top to bottom. She may not have the slightest interest in sport (save for the World Cup when her favourite pastime is to ogle at the legs of the beautiful Adonis-like Italians), yet her life is dominated by it. Thank goodness I'm no longer off racing twice a week – that would never do.

My wife is perhaps not the only one to be severely trauma-tised by Mr Robert Grillo. I have two younger brothers, only one of whom can claim to live a perfectly normal life. The youngest, Manny, cannot. Some ten years my junior (there-fore not around to witness my formative years as a saddo), he needed a role model, and I was it. Lucky boy. Once able to read with a fair degree of competence he seized upon my diligently compiled chart book. Over a period of a couple of years I had kept meticulous records of the UK and American singles and album music charts. These were the league tables of the music industry, so it was no surprise that I took to making detailed and precise records of what was happening on the music scene.

Manny was not yet out of infant school but that particular compilation of the banal was regarded as his finest reading material. He dribbled all over it, several charts were rendered unreadable due to the smudged felt pen which resulted, but he nonetheless developed a rather amusing party piece. He could recite the exact weekly chart positions of every eighties hit single by the time he was ten years of age. I, of course, have to take credit for this and for his scoring maximum marks on Ken Bruce's 'popmaster' on Radio Two not very long ago. In recent times there has been more than one occasion when we have gone for a night out on the tiles and he has put a pound in a pop quiz machine and won enough money to buy our drinks all evening.

It is perhaps sad, then, that Manny has never really taken too much of interest in the fine details associated with football league tables, although I am, under threat of torture, unable to mention here the precise details of his victory over the Mayoress of Bournemouth on Channel 4's *Countdown* in 1994.

I have to put it on record too that, as far as I am aware, no former girlfriends have gone on to develop symptoms of the anal retention that they have been subjected to. There were times when they had to take a back seat to what was going on at the local playing fields, but the majority were surprisingly patient. One of them spent her Saturday afternoons fulfilling the role of scorer at her local cricket club – maybe I could have made more use of those facts and figures she helped to compile. Another has subsequently become as obsessively devoted to long-distance running as I was in my day, while another had no interest in sport of any kind but experienced such a relentless succession of jobs during our short time together that I could have written a full statistical analysis of her greatest failures.

Now, of course, there is the girlfriend who, with amazing fortitude, became my wife. The family and the in-laws also show remarkable resilience in the face of adversity. The mother-in-law often asks me 'When are you going to write about something interesting?' or 'Does anyone actually buy your books?' Of course they do.

I do worry about form 11RG at Greenhead High School, however. They are currently my form group, for the fifth year in succession, and one or two of them are beginning to show symptoms that suggest they have been spending far too much time in the presence of an anorak. They stopped asking me which team I supported a long time ago, once they had realised that I wasn't joking when I said it was currently Silsden FC, and they now very rarely discuss the weekend's Premier League results with each other. Their first words on a Monday morning are 'How did they get on?' A few of the lads no longer need to ask me that, they sit with me at Cougar Park in Keighley. They could be jumping on a bus or train and making the relatively short journey to Valley Parade, Turf Moor or, God help them, Elland Road. But no, they happily pay their £2.50 and watch their local North West Counties League fare. They may grow out of it, but I have my doubts.

Robert Mulderrig, Oliver Holder, Tom Robinson and Ryan Stewart all play for Long Lee Juniors FC, and not surprisingly they all aspire to become professional footballers when they grow older (I hope they do). Robert's elder brother Sean doesn't. He wants to be a Premier League referee instead. I haven't once heard them talk about playing for Bradford City,

Liverpool or Burnley. They sit in the main stand at Cougar Park, week in, week out, talking about how they will manage to turn results around when they break into the Silsden first team. Lovely. I could be paying good money to see these lads play in a few years time. The offer of a free cup of tea for any lad or lass in my form group going to watch a game featuring Silsden Football Club could very soon begin to reap dividends.

It seems the boys' parents are happy for them to spend time on the terraces at their local soccer ground. It does keep them off the streets, after all, although it brings a whole new dimension to the term 'hanging out with a strange crowd'. Not one of them has yet shown signs of wanting to attend away matches too – although if they did I'm sure 'Lost in Barrow' would be more than happy to help them out with train times. A couple of them are keen to find out what the official attendance is, if only to work out what percentage of the crowd is made up of Greenhead students. They will be coming armed with pocket notebooks next. Tom claims that one of his favourite TV celebrities is John Motson. Yes, the signs are there. They have even suggested bringing a drum to home matches in order to create a little more atmosphere. They turned up at one high-profile fixture wearing 'Grillo's Barmy Army' T-shirts. From tiny acorns…

Not everyone in 11RG is a football fanatic. 'Of all the form tutors we could have got landed with, we get this geek,' complains Nassreen. 'Who the flip would want to read about the things you write about?' others add. Good question.

There are others who have been afflicted in different ways. I am as enthusiastic in a classroom as I am on the terraces at my local football club. You can make geography a pretty boring subject if you really want – the Model of Demographic Transition really can be a bind for GCSE students unless you make it sound fun. And it can be. 'You're a geek sir, and you aren't even forty yet. That's not right.'

Pity, then, poor Nayar, now happily enjoying the benefits of dentistry at some far-flung university. Nayar was a particularly colourful character, keen, enthusiastic and one of the more lateral thinkers in her group. She also claims that I ruined her life. 'I went to the seaside with my family,' she complains, 'and all I can think about is longshore drift and stacks and bloody stumps. I tried explaining to my dad how hydraulic action contributes to the erosion of our coastline around Holderness. I just got laughed at.'

Nayar once wrote a piece of love poetry about coastal erosion, so she really knows her stuff. Others are beginning to show similar symptoms. I am regularly accosted in the school dining hall by equally inane students who ask me if I am 'voluntarily taking a temporarily internal migration' to another part of the school building. Of course I am – if it were not voluntary I would be a refugee. I must be making it interesting if the kids are thinking geography outside the classroom, but I wonder whether I am creating a generation of nerds. On second thoughts, my conclusion is always the same – definitely not. If you met these kids you would appreciate their amazing sense of humour and their ability to actually have a laugh while they are learning. After all, you remember very little if you are bored senseless, but you remember far more if you enjoy what you are doing, and this lot go to prove that you can be geeky, but you can be a good laugh as well.

When you are a little left of centre the younger kids will believe anything you tell them. Knowing of my overriding obsession for sport they were taken in by one slightly eccentric English teacher and good friend of mine, Gary Kaye. One of the world's most talented wind-up merchants, Kaye informed one year-seven group that I had been on the books of Bradford City FC when they were promoted to the Premier League in 1999. Allegedly, upon their elevation to the top flight they terminated my contract because I was deemed not to possess the necessary skills for the job. Unfortunately, once rumours start they are hard to stop, and I only narrowly managed to intercept a hastily prepared student petition to have me reinstated.

Revenge was sweet. Kaye is a particularly well-built lad, so it was a little tricky explaining that he was not absent from work with a bout of flu, but had in fact been arrested in Nottingham city centre only hours earlier. He had been driving down to an ice-skating competition that would hopefully mark his comeback in that particular sport following the last Winter Olympics when he dropped his partner. Unfortunately, his car broke down and he was forced to walk the last half-mile to the arena wearing nothing but his tight purple leotard, hence his resultant detention in the local police cells. Again, only hasty action prevented a student uprising. If you have an eccentric sense of humour then the kids will believe you every time.

My form group at my last school got the bug too. Not for Silsden Football Club, or for falling for far-fetched and made-up tales, but for writing those books that surely no one else would ever want to read. Faced with copies of my first ever book, there was only one page they were interested in.

It was entitled 'About the Author'. They thought this section of the book particularly funny, although they were happy to learn that I did have a life outside school: I had dogs, a girl-friend (the future Mrs Grillo) and I went to university. This had a lasting effect. English lessons were never the same: they all wanted to write a book and they willingly took work home to complete – unheard of in this particular part of Bradford. Surely a good thing.

At least it seemed a good thing. You only had to read their 'stories'. Half a side of A4, rushed, without punctuation or properly constructed sentences, and with very little thought put into it. However, on the back of the sheet, and continued on one or more pages, was a very well constructed piece from each 'about the author', and they tended to go like this:

> Gemma is thirteen years old and lives at home with her mum, three brothers, two sisters and three stepsisters. She has recently moved to a new flat where she hopes her front door won't be covered in graffiti. She will soon be reunited with her dad, who has done time for armed robbery. This might mean that uncle Jim will have to move out.

It is perhaps a blessing then that I no longer teach English. Geography provides less opportunity for the hidden anorak in you to reveal itself, unless you are in 11RG and you know exactly where Ramsbottom, and Stone, and Atherton, and Ashton under Lyme, and Ashton in Makerfield are.

The current staff at Greenhead prefer to humour my ten-dency towards the unconventional. At times, they can often be quite amusing. The first time I received copies of my own books as gifts in our annual 'secret santa bran tub' was quite amusing, the second, third and fourth times slightly less so.

You must not forget then that the common household anorak has friends and family. You may even be one of those loyal friends, or a partner subjected to fact after useless fact, routine after boring routine. There is no need to worry; he is not the only one of his kind out there. He is happy to do what he does in his own world, but it does not mean that he loves you less, or prefers his hobby to you, he loves you dearly, you are still number one in his life, but he is one of those people who just happens to live in his own world for at least part of the day. Do not pity him, please try to understand him, because he really is quite normal.

Chapter Seven

FOOTBALL MANAGER

Most football fans can do a far better job than the referee. After all, most refs are useless, most of them have dodgy eyesight, several are just plain stupid and the others are of questionable parentage. The linesmen, or referees assistants as they are known these days, are not much better. And then there is the manager. He is undoubtedly the most derided individual in the game after the officials, particularly when his team is struggling at the foot of the table. After all, you would not have made that substitution, or you would have made it half an hour earlier, your left-winger has done nothing to justify his place in the team, and what on earth is the season's leading scorer doing on the bench?

A first teaching job in Bradford enabled me to do what I had always had something of a longing for; that is to manage my very own team. Grillo's Gallopers may have existed only in my own imagination but here was an opportunity to not only manage a team, but be chairman, coach and club statistician at the same time.

Woodside Middle School football teams had played sporadic fixtures over the previous few years, but in 1991

Mr Rob Grillo had other plans. Despite being the smallest school of its type in the district, this newly qualified teacher and his bunch of merry men were about to embark on an unheralded run of success that would inevitably result in the under-11s football team becoming the very top side of its kind in the country. The under-13s and girls would do the same a year later. Or so I hoped.

In reality, the under-11s team were nothing special, neither were the under-12s nor the girls' sides, all of whom tried their hardest but were never going to set the world alight. For almost a decade, life in this part of the world revolved around these sports teams. This was because the teacher in charge was an anorak, completely obsessed with what he had created. He was crap at the game himself but as keen as hell to provide some statistics for us all to talk about.

Local rivals Mandale provided the first opposition for the new Woodside under-11s, in their brand spanking new blue and white shirts. For some reason we had an agreement to play the game in four quarters, but at least the game was at home, at the 'Woodside Stadium', the school field that was overlooked at the time by half a dozen council flats. There was not one person in that city more nervous than myself before that game. I prepared for days, I devised a master plan, I primed my team – training twice a week – and I primed them again. I left no stone unturned, and I might as well have been on the field of play with them. As it was, I teetered on the touchline, verging on a nervous breakdown and making myself hoarse. The match was organised for the benefit of one person – me. The kids from both teams enjoyed a tremendous game, those parents that attended had a jolly good time, the opposing manager – who happily agreed to referee the match – left happy, but there was not one of them who experienced the sense of utter fulfilment that I was feeling at that time. I felt every tackle, experienced an overwhelming euphoria as Woodside went in front, a resounding sense of relief as the same set of lads clawed their way back to 2-2 in the dying moments, and an immense pleasure as they celebrated their first match together at the final whistle. Michael Beck and Stephen Smith scored the first ever Woodside goals for their new manager. They may not remember that fact but I do.

Over the next few seasons every single match was meticulously logged. Every scoreline and goalscorer was recorded in my little green notebook alongside every team line-up. Every pupil had easy access to this data, which was presented neatly on the display boards specially erected outside my classroom. There were times when boys had to be given a shove, cajoled into going to their lessons or threatened with detention if they did not move on. This was the most important notice board for miles and it contained everything you could ever want to know about football at this particular school. And Mr Rob Grillo compiled it.

After a couple of years playing regular friendly fixtures, I took the plunge and entered my under-13s into the Bradford Schools League for the first time. We would have suffered a mauling by the bigger and better established schools, so we were placed in the bottom tier, the 'supplementary' or 'third' division. Even then it was a struggle at times, not to field a full complement of players because, despite the small size of the school, there was never any shortage of girls and boys wanting to play, but to earn a priceless victory against just as eager and much larger opponents. We quickly discovered that this division was no pushover – world domination would have to wait even longer.

Every single match had its moments, not always pleasant ones, but there was always something to talk about in school the following day. There was the occasion of my star centre forward, my leading goalscorer by a mile, walking off the field with five minutes to play because he had failed to score for the first time that season. We were 6-0 up and he sulked. He just threw his shirt in my direction and stomped off home. To give the lad credit, he did write a carefully composed apology afterwards to the coach of the opposing team, and apologised to the rest of the school in assembly. He was forgiven and went on to score many more goals for me that season. Any sensible football coach would have banned him for the rest of the season for such insolence but it would have ruined my master plan; we were in the middle of a good run at the time and I was damned if I was going to lose my star striker! Impartiality? Bah humbug!

On a different note, there was the dramatic conclusion to an epic 5-5 draw at home to Wellington before that. We trailed 0-5 at the break, completely outplayed and outfought, second to every ball and poor in practically every part of the field. The second-half comeback was one of the most sensational of all time, at least in this part of the city. The all-important equaliser come eight seconds into injury time, just as the Wellington coach was politely asking me when I was going to blow my whistle for full time. The lads may as well have won the FA Cup, there were tears shed by at least one parent, and there was the never-to-be forgotten complaint from another: 'We would have won that game if you'd disallowed all their goals for offside.' Yep, I was the partially sighted referee, devoid of any modicum of common sense. We had somehow managed to fight back from the brink of defeat and yet there was still no pleasing some people.

Parents can be your best allies in this game, completely supportive of everything you are doing following yet another rout in the rain. The best of them offer lifts in their cars, bring half-time food and drinks, offer to clean the kits and generally put themselves out to help in any way they can. But others can become your Achilles heel, particularly if they consider their young protégé to be the best thing since George Best. Every defeat is down to the coach, their child's every miss is due to them not having been taught properly, they should be playing for Manchester United but the Manchester United coach hasn't spotted them yet for some reason, and so on. Then there are the plain stupid ones. I remember one lady turning up just five minutes before a game and marching her son off because she was having her hair done and she needed someone to look after the little 'uns.

Of course some of them could have done a far better job than I was trying to do. For example, the taxi driver whose son was in the team tried subtle hints while escorting me to a city-centre nightclub. 'I'd play three at the back, which would give us more attacking options.' Us? They were my team, their raison d'être was to provide enjoyment and a huge number of statistics for me, and for me only.

There were many incidents that were duly noted in that green book that roused a smile, and others that resulted in many a head buried in the hands of a stressed-out sports teacher. I lost my keys during one match. They had my whistle attached. I ran around like a headless chicken, I blamed all and sundry. I made myself hoarse (again) trying to shout my decisions, and right on full time I found them in the centre circle. The following week I refused to allow one of my under-13s to go to the toilet halfway through the second half. He could wait, the game was evenly poised. He couldn't wait, if only he had told me he had diarrhoea. I had to let him go, but the incident had by then run its course and the rest of the team had to play around the offending puddle.

Some incidents were a little more light-hearted. What football team hasn't played a game where a local dog has interrupted proceedings? Ours showed a neat touch before deflecting a fourth goal past my hapless goalkeeper. Luckily, the match was not evenly poised. We conceded another four after that, none of them accountable to our four-legged friend.

I was once shouted at by a dear old lady who took exception to the footballers who had turned up to play a match on their pitch. How dare they spoil her walk? The dog crapped on the halfway line. I think I preferred the one that scored goals, at least it didn't leave a lasting impression on the boots of potential young superstars.

Others have invaded our fixtures too. A teenage motorcyclist paid us a visit once. I don't think it was his bike, as he was in an awful rush and there was an awful lot of shouting going on at the other end of the field. This was Woodside after all. If someone steals your bike, you steal it back the following day.

I have been felled by a particularly hard shot on goal. It was my own silly fault for being in the wrong place. I defy any referee to tell me that they have not suffered a similar humiliation at one time in their life. I was also invited for tea a couple of times after taking home one of my team after a match. Being the professional that I am, I was forced to turn down these delightful offers, no matter how attractive the young lady – whether parent or elder sister – offering such hospitality may have been.

The school football teams soon became an addiction. Before I knew it I had three boys' teams and one girls' team in the local schools league, and on top of that various five- and six-a-side competitions to play for. It was becoming a bit too much. Step forward Neil Smith, a newly qualified round teacher who shared the same enthusiasm for the job, and for Woodside Middle School FC. He lacked the eccentric obsession that I had, but no matter, he came on board in the mid-nineties and between us we created a master plan.

We organised up to three games per week before the dark nights set in. I took charge of the under-13s and the girls, while he had responsibility for the under-11s and -12s. We refereed each other's matches, organised training camps, and gave our better players the chance to shine against older boys when we got the chance. The school football players became celebrities on their own estate. Basically, they became quite good at what they did, and it improved their self-esteem in the classroom and outside of school, as well as improving relationships in school on what is a tough estate. They went home and talked about their exciting matches and their brilliant goals, and for the first time they had something to be proud of. And Woodside responded.

Suddenly, we were faced with crowd problems. The school field was located right in the centre of the estate. Those arriving home from work would drive past a packed ground, and would want to get in on the act. When I say packed, I mean it. On occasions there was not a space to be had on the touchline, apart from behind each goal. Others would hang out of the windows of their flats, and friends and relatives would join them. The more important fixtures created what can only be described as a frenzy, and things came to a head when the under-13s reached the quarter-finals of the Bradford Schools Cup. A fortnight earlier they had defeated a school from a higher league in the last minute of extra time in front of a particularly partisan home following, and suddenly the locals were hooked. There were telephone calls to the school office requesting details of the next match, parents who had previously never shown their faces inside the building suddenly appeared and acted as if you had always been their best mate, and even the rest of the staff took interest. This was unheralded.

The tie itself was as one-sided as it could have been and proved a huge anticlimax. Our opponents, Manningham, were a class apart. They led by a single goal at the break, and once the second went in soon after the interval all hell broke loose. The home crowd wanted blood. Shouts of 'kick 'im' and 'break 'is legs' became the norm, and the home team players responded, they did kick their opponents, who merely upped their game and scored five more. I blew the final whistle five minutes early, I could take no more, and both teams had had enough. Luckily, our opponents were not harmed, although their minibus had its tyres let down, and I needed to have a rethink. I also had apologies to make the following morning.

So we moved. All of 400 yards. There are not many school football teams who have to move grounds due to excessive interest in their home fixtures, but there was one right here. Luckily, at the time I lived next door to the groundsman of the nearby Horsfall playing fields. Behind the running track and home of Bradford Park Avenue FC are a number of pitches that are used by local Sunday league teams, so he allowed us to play our home games there instead, although as we were using the pitches free of charge we couldn't use the changing or showering facilities there. He did provide us with goal nets and corner flags, though, as ours had been 'borrowed' one night after we forgot to take them down after a match. Our new pitch was a mere five minutes' walk from our changing rooms at school, though, and as most other schools arrived changed, there were no problems.

The rogue elements of Woodside's support did not reappear at Horsfall so things were able to continue as normal, at least for a short while. The statto in me was getting restless and needed a new challenge, so along came the match-day programme. Not a cheap and nasty last-minute effort, though, but one that detailed the full story of the season so far.

I now spent more time working on this than I did planning my lessons, and by now the school had endured a torrid OFSTED inspection. Following the removal of the old head, we had been placed in special measures, so I should really have concerned myself with dealing with that instead. Surely the reputation of the school was paramount? But no, I now had another outlet for my never-ending output of useless facts and figures.

I encouraged the students to compose match reports, and had no end of helpers putting the thing together. Staff took action snaps for the programme, and the photocopier in the school office needed new ink cartridges far more regularly as production exceeded thirty for some games. The programme was featured in the local press, and we came fourth in the Schools and Youth Clubs section in the prestigious Wirral Programme Awards. We then had to deal with requests for back copies from all over the UK. Now this was getting silly. Although the school's profile was being raised considerably, what had started as one man's obsession was beginning to get out of hand.

I had volunteered to help out on the Bradford Schools FA Committee by now, and took on the role of results secretary for the under-13s boys' leagues. This was schoolboy football for heaven's sake! Somehow, I can assure you, I did find the time to teach. I now compiled league tables – I was in heaven. (I also compiled league tables for my form group based on how many subject 'merits' they had been awarded during the term – nothing whatsoever to do with sport but at least a means of using what skills I had in the pursuit of the formation of irrelevant statistics).

The role also served as some recompense for my never having established myself in my own school football team. Rod Farnell had given me seven minutes in goal for Grange School's first ever under-11's match. I made a right prat of myself. Nobody had told me that the 'keeper was only allowed five steps with the ball in his hand. I got a lift to that match from one of my mates, and he compounded my misery by telling me afterwards that his mum had called me a 'know-all', merely because I knew more than he did about football.

During the next three years I played twice more for the school team, both times because our first-, second- and third-choice goalkeepers were all unavailable. In the first game I was forced to play centre forward after the break because our captain hurt his leg, and as we only had ten men he went in goal himself. I never got close to scoring, and our opponents, the perennial whipping boys, went on to defeat us 2-1.

My final appearance was the one that ended my career. We were two up at the break and coasting to victory. With only ten minutes remaining I fumbled a high cross and Roy Mason of Highfield School tapped home as I lay prostrate. Not thirty seconds later the same player fired home a volley to equalise. I never even saw the ball as it cruised into the back of the net, and I never played again. We won 3-2 that day but I made the decision never again to try to pretend to be a decent footballer, because I wasn't.

Less than a decade later, and as a school football coach, I was again involved in the game. I was not quite the infamous Brian Glover character in *Kes*, for the simple reason that, for a start, the kids were far better at the sport than I was, and I would never have pretended to be Manchester United's ace striker as Glover would have liked to have been. I would have been a Bradford City centre forward instead. There was still the odd Glover-like individual knocking around the playing fields of Bradford at the time, though, treating each schoolboy match as if it were his last. Every decision would be disputed and every goal celebrated as if he had scored it himself. It's not just the parents that are prone to do that.

I was not the only eccentric among these people, and of course I was not the only over-enthusiastic one among them. Maybe they lacked the unhealthy approach to irrelevant statistics that I had, but some of the guys who ran their school football teams were keen as hell. You could be sure that the first telephone call of the new term would be from he who considered his team to have the best chance of winning the league. He was keen to get all his fixtures arranged at the earliest possible convenience, and who can blame him? If you were stuck for transport you could be sure that he would provide you with his own school's minibus, and he would drive it himself. There was nothing wrong with that, I would have done the same had Woodside been up there with the best.

Among the other characters, there was the old-timer, the laid-back cigar-smoking gentleman seeing out the remaining years of his eventful career. Seen on the touchline week in, week out in his tweed suit, he is happy just to fulfil the necessary fixtures and provide his charges with the recreation they desire. Of course, standards have fallen since he started teaching, but he is a gentle bloke, full of tales of the past and more than happy for you to use nine extra substitutes in order give all your lads a run-out. You could be 12-0 up or 12-0 down, he is just as affable either way.

There is the enthusiastic, newly qualified team manager, the ones who would happily arrange a tiddlywinks competition if you suggested it. His team plays the Dutch way – total football – and will usually be six up at the interval. He will then put on his star player, usually an eleven-year-old girl, and she will rip you to shreds in the same way that her sister did in the first half. Contrast this with the hippy type, who turns up with a team of thirty-six in order to give them all a game. He has to do this because he is off to Nepal next week – the head has somehow allowed him leave of absence – so he won't be able to fulfil any more fixtures for a while. He rewards his leading scorer by putting him in goal in order to allow some-one else to take the glory, and he offers to give your substitutes a game for his lot should you decide not to play them yourself. He will ask you the score at half-time either because he just wasn't watching or because a parent has just turned up and, although he does not believe in keeping tabs of the score, this particular parent is keen to know whether his charges are, in fact, winning or on the end of a real hiding.

I met each one of these individuals. They did exist. They were just as obsessive as I was, and it made what I was doing all the more justifiable. Get yourself off to your nearest schools football match and you too can go sports teacher spotting.

Then it was all over. Bradford Education decided to abandon its three-tier system and the middle schools were to be abolished. They were shutting us down. Did they not know what we were doing in this not-so-quiet backwater? Neil Smith and I decided to go out with a bang rather than a whimper. We extended our training sessions, organised more matches and took our charges to the peak of their fitness. There were more statistics than ever before to compile, and it completed our adventure.

Suddenly, we had not one but two successful sides to deal with. The under-11 boys, backed by the best set of parents you could ask for, were no longer the whipping boys of the league, and they won more matches than they lost. The under-13s enjoyed their most exciting season ever. I knew all too well how every side in their league was getting on – I was results secretary after all, and it was a joy to compile a weekly league table that saw Woodside Middle School on top. We had some frights along the way: a 3-1 victory over

Hutton – our first ever victory over this lot – was endured as they laid siege to the Woodside goal for an entire second half. We came from behind to defeat bottom-of-the-table Holme 4-3 in the dying seconds of the game, but we stayed there, at the very top, until our final match of the season against Great Horton. As we had just dragged ourselves out of OFSTED's special measures, they had fallen in, so it was nice to see that, like us, their football team was flying the flag for them. We lost 1-2. Ahead at the break, we had one hand on the supplementary league title, but we were turned over in the second half by the better team. It was agony for Neil too, who played a blinder in the middle, but I was proud. We may have so been close, yet finished the season with nothing, but what had been created was a huge oak tree that had started from the smallest of acorns.

For the record, Woodside Middle School's record victory was achieved away from home – a 12-0 rout of Holme Middle on 15 April 1999. It was an under-11 boys fixture and the coach of our opponents had banned his under-11s from playing due to poor behaviour in the classroom, so he fielded his under-10s instead. One of our lads scored a double hat-trick that afternoon.

Our record defeat was suffered little over one year later, in our final fixture before closure. An under-13 eight-a-side girls team travelled a couple of miles up the road to play county champions Mandale – ironically, the school's first ever opponents in the Grillo era. We lost 0-17. A Premier League manager would have been sacked after a result like that, but the Woodside girls cared not. They enjoyed themselves, got very muddy and went home with a bag of chips each.

Horsfall playing fields exist now as they did then, but the old school field, where it all started, was last being used as a rugby field for the local junior club. The flats that overlooked the 'Woodside Stadium' have been bulldozed, and pleasant semi-detached houses line the street instead.

As I moved on, to Greenhead High School back home in Keighley, I left a little piece of me behind on those playing fields in south Bradford. I had a brief stint in charge of one team at my new place, but it wasn't the same and I left that job to the PE staff, who could no doubt do a far better job than I.

There is little doubt that I was in my element running school football teams. There can be no denying that I was an anorak, I had an obsessive interest in the games themselves, they were as important to me as the teaching was, and I spent far more time working out what my next move would be with this than plotting what to do next with the gorgeous cleaning lady I was seeing behind her fella's back. She provided another pleasant distraction nonetheless, and for some time the act of teaching itself was relegated to third place in my list of priorities.

Regardless of my own obsessions, hundreds of girls and boys benefited from Woodside Middle School's football teams, countless parents shivered in the cold and experienced the same emotions as their kids, and two sports teachers (one of whom actually taught science) had the time of their lives. I think deep down I also wanted to do what Rod Farnell had done all those years earlier. It was his enthusiasm for his sports teams that lit the spark in me, and I'm sure he would have been proud had he been around to witness this.

I still have the complete record of all the fixtures we played somewhere in the attic. They lie alongside those of the other sporting events I went on to organise, for my own pleasure, of course – the school cross-country races in the farmer's fields opposite the school and the South Bradford Schools cross-country championships at Horsfall playing fields. What an anorak. One day, somewhere, somebody might want to research this.

There are those in the world of grass-roots football who know exactly how I felt every week on that touchline. They may not be as useless as I have always been at football – and are quite often former players themselves – but they have lived every moment with their team as if they were on that pitch themselves. They are as obsessed with their unpaid role as I ever was and would do it all again if they had to start at the beginning.

Silsden's Andy Geary can identify with all of that, as can Roy Mason, that Highfield Middle School centre forward who put two goals past me in the space of a minute many years back. As Mason reached the twilight of his career, like many other before him, he became a manager himself. After two decades of success in county and district league football he took the plunge, and is now firmly established as head boy at Summerhill Lane, the home of Steeton Football Club – or head anorak as those at the club would prefer to call him. Now this doesn't surprise me. Of all the lads at Greenhead Grammar School in the early 1980s, he was the one who would always take his interest beyond the mere playing of the game.

He was no different from the other lads during his forma-tive years, though. As a small lad he would go down to his local rec straight after school and play until it was dark. These were the days when it was still safe to do that. The fact that he was one of the youngest lads to play on Keighley's renowned Burgess Field was not going to deter a young Mason, and being barred from playing with a proper football at junior school also failed to dent his enthusiasm:

> I used to go to the shop before school and buy a Jiff and just squirt the juice straight out. A full one was too heavy and could break a window. I'm sure that the shopkeeper couldn't believe his eyes when he saw me and the lads doing that. The Jiffs were great for improving your ball skills; they rolled all over the place and were difficult to control.

A fourteen-year-old Roy Mason then went on to form his own football team. He wasn't happy with what the local clubs were offering so he founded Springfield Rovers, an informal side based around the lads he went to school with, and named after the street where he lived. They were informal to everyone except Mason; within days of their formation the entire team had been forced to exchange a fiver for the yellow and blue football shirts that he had procured. I don't think that was in their original contracts. After one friendly fixture on a now long-disused pitch adjacent to the local tennis club, Rovers floundered through lack of interest. No lack of interest from Mason, who was by now out of pocket, but from the others who were not quite ready to share their leader's aspirations of taking the world by storm. He had been owner, manager, captain and director of his first venture, and he certainly wasn't put off by its apparent failure.

Mason subsequently became heavily involved in the running of every club he played for. He produced a fanzine for his first Sunday league club, and revelled in the dual role of player-chairman at Keighley Phoenix FC before family commitments forced him to give up his role on the committee. His absence from the boardroom was only a temporary phenomenon, however, once he had thrown in his lot with his local village club. At Steeton he has at one time filled every position on the field, bar keeping goal, and after one season in charge of the reserves is now a popular man at the helm of the club's first team. Luckily for him, this particular set-up is no Springfield Rovers, it is most definitely not a one-man show, and he has a huge backing from not only his fellow club officials, but also his players. They get their kits for free now, you see.

You only have to turn to the first page in the club's matchday programme to see how utterly professional he likes things to be. 'Mason's Message' always extends a warm welcome to visiting players, officials and supporters and goes on to review the highlights of the previous week's matches, training sessions and transfer gossip. You could be mistaken in thinking you were reading about a team in the higher echelons of the non-League game here. But this is the West Riding County Amateur League – a step up from your average local league fare but light years away from the Football Conference that heads the non-League pyramid.

Read on and it is obvious that Roy Mason also assumes the unofficial title of head scout, and there cannot be a junior-team manager in the district who has not had that phone call from Mason asking for potential bright new recruits for Steeton's senior set-up. 'This may only be the County Amateur League but a club is going to go nowhere if it is not run properly,' he proclaims. 'It is my ambition to have a fantastic youth set-up just as good as the one down the road at Silsden,' he says, acknowledging Steeton's rivals as the team to which all other Keighley sides aspire. 'We cannot even think about progressing up the non-League ladder without one.'

Steeton are certainly beginning to get themselves noticed, not least due to their recently introduced match-day programme. Mason is quick to acknowledge its appeal: 'We have had 'hoppers from as far afield as Bedford and Edinburgh who sought us out merely to get hold of a copy.' My bet is that they also had a new ground to tick off too – we know all about those people.

There is more than a passing resemblance between Steeton's man at the top and Chelsea's recent manager, Jose Mourinho. The Portuguese millionaire does look strangely similar to Roy Mason, although probably has far fewer injuries to his squad to worry about at key stages in the season. Mason's nickname is 'Jose', and he is sponsored by Steeton Top Barbers, so I suspect the grey sideburns may be fashioned in honour of his better-known counterpart rather than the other way round.

Mason's role at work has also led him to appear on the shopping channel, modelling his company's finest wears, alongside Gloria Hunniford. I was sceptical when I first heard this claim, but a little research led me to conclude that Mason, and the anoraks he has adorned on national television, have indeed shared screen space with Ireland's first lady.

There is little indication that Mason is slowing down or tiring of his crusade to make Steeton the undisputed kings of world football, and his enthusiasm extends to the club's social activities too. 'Organising a pub quiz or race night at the Goats Head is quite easy with Mason around,' quips one member of his first-team squad, 'except that it isn't really. Roy will always lend a hand if you ask, but if you don't ask and you don't get it sorted quickly he will lend a hand anyway, and do a bloody good job of it too'.

He may not yet be as successful as Andy Geary at Silsden, but there is no doubting that Roy has every chance of achieving just as much as his friend.

'I am pleased to say that my ten-year-old son is showing signs of following in his dad's footsteps both on the field and also as an anorak,' Mason is proud to announce. 'Sharon, my long-suffering wife, can often be heard saying, "You're becoming as sad as your Dad!" – which I take as a compliment.' Roy Mason's interest in his chosen sport must be pretty obsessive if Mrs Mason is complaining. She comes from a well-known local sporting family so is used to the trials and tribulations of living with a fanatic. Roy is just that bit special!

Every good manager has his collection of telephone numbers, those of the players in his squad and those he would just love to have in his squad. Again, Mason is no different, but he has his other collections too. It all started with his Panini football sticker collection. Mason was far more addicted than anyone else, and he still proudly boasts a fully intact 1978 collection in his loft. At least, he hopes it is in his loft.

Since then, he has gone on to collect football badges, and his occupation as an overseas footwear buyer for a mail-order company has enabled him to build up a fine collection of international pennants to go with his domestic ones. He is really proud of these. Of course, Mason could just have easily chosen to collect Baines Shields or final league tables.

As a final point, do not be surprised if Roy Mason junior follows in his father's footsteps. This young chap plays for Silsden (not as easy a task as it sounds, because his dad referees home games), but don't be surprised if he too forms his own club some time in the near future. He may one day be in the main stand at some non-League football ground, discussing the pressing local sporting issues with Ian Robinson's lads.

Chapter Eight

ANORAKS I HAVE KNOWN

We all know somebody who likes to do something that is may be a little different from the norm. Take me for example, I like to run into work at least once a week – a pleasant six-and-a-half-mile journey along the pleasant scenery of the river Worth and its accompanying scenery – before crawling in through the front gates at the same time as the first students are arriving. Most of them are still half asleep and lacking any of the motivation I have just shown over the past forty-five minutes. I also like to run back home at the end of the same day. Colleagues consider this a little daft, while the kids just think of it as plain stupid. After all, I do have a car. Why would I want to leave it at home? I tried to explain that I was just doing my bit for the environment by not using my car every day, but this just didn't wash – and anyway, Mrs Grillo would refute that as she claims that the local environment is harmed enormously by the unpleasant aroma emanating from my tired body when I return home.

Many of my work colleagues, as well as the students, have a hard time understanding why I would prefer to watch a little-known football team along with just a few other souls, when instead I could be watching the superstars that play for Manchester United or Liverpool. Others would understand a little more if I supported Bradford City instead, as one or two of my colleagues currently still do, but Silsden, why on earth would I pay good money to watch Silsden?

You know by now why I pay good money to watch Silsden Football Club. I have gone to great lengths to argue that the average anorak, such as myself, is not as pathetically sad as many assume, but there are one or two who, even I acknowledge, really are quite worrying.

Ventus and Yeadon Celtic – a football club based in north Leeds – know all about such individuals. Several years ago they became one of a growing list of West Yorkshire clubs to have their very own match-day programme. Except that they knew nothing about it. It is alleged that a local gent, who had already earned himself something of a reputation down in the south-west of the country, and who I believe I may have met on numerous occasions, decided that it was about time this local club had their own programme. So he kindly produced it for them. He also produced similar efforts for other household names such as Pudsey Liberals and Skipton LMS FC. It is not clear whether these clubs were indeed party to these publications, but it did create rather a lot of interest among groundhoppers.

This chap really was sad. The programmes were, in many cases, well produced and very factual, but it did not take you long to realise that here was a very obsessive man. League tables tell us which teams are at the top of the league, they show us which teams are struggling and which have games in hand, and they enable us to spend much of our spare time working out all permutations of what could happen in the near future. Looking back over tables from our dim and distant past, we can see exactly how the likes of VAW Low Moor and Skipton LMS went on in their respective leagues. League tables should be easy to read. Therefore, when VAW are referred to as 'Veretingte Aluminium Werke Low Moor', and Skipton as 'Skipton London Midland and Scottish Railway' in these tables, then that really is too much information. It is a trifle too obsessive.

Tim Welsh – a fellow schoolteacher – is an anorak, and he's obsessive, but certainly not as bizarre as the gentleman above. Tim loves his football. And his cricket. And the facts and figures that go with it. Not content with fulfilling the dual role of player-secretary and treasurer of Brontë Wanderers FC – local rivals to Roy Mason's Steeton FC – which is time-consuming enough, he has also enjoyed a distinguished career with his local cricket club, Haworth West End. There are two cricket clubs in Haworth – Haworth CC, who play on a lovely and partially sheltered meadow on the edge of the Brontë village, and West End, who play home fixtures right on top of the hill above Haworth. It is as exposed and bleak as you could ever wish for. This is Yorkshire – we get nine-month winters followed by three months of rain up here, especially on top of exposed hills. Yet Welsh was more than happy to endure the driving gales, the horizontal rain and the freezing temperatures for over a decade. And he did not stop there. Cricket matches involve statistics: the batting and bowling averages, the run-rates, leg-byes and googlies to catalogue – Tim Welsh would happily reel them off for all and sundry, week after week in the summer. His favourite book is *Wisden*'s cricket annual. He actually reads each edition; he does not merely use it as a point of reference. When most kiddies of his era were discovering Enid Blyton, or J.R.R. Tolkein, Welsh was discovering *Wisden*, he was reading it for a purpose at the age of ten. I fully expect him to produce a full statistical history of league and club cricket in Keighley and district in the very near future and I will be the first to buy a copy. A case of the eccentric history teacher maybe, but this one certainly doesn't wear the tweed jacket with imitation leather elbow patches.

Schoolteachers make very good anoraks. They make good listeners too. Eric Sykes was the head at my former school, Woodside, and he really was a tremendously funny guy. He was also my mentor in my probationary year as a teacher, and a damn good friend. He listened well, he did not share even the remotest interest in sport of any kind, and his school PE report once stated: 'Eric makes limited use of his limited ability.'

This did not prevent him from being an anorak, however. An immensely popular fellow among his peers and charges, Sykes could play the piano – an essential trait if you are a male and wish to progress up the ladder in the primary sector (which is why I subsequently went secondary) – and for as long as he remembers he has been a bus enthusiast. Yes, a bus enthusiast. I know not of the term that is applied to the bus enthusiast, but I do know that an obsession with public transport bears very little resemblance to that of the sport enthusiast. But we understood each other's 'situation', as you might call it. Eric like myself, led a very fruitful social life and had plenty of friends. He would take himself off for a weekend on the buses, travelling the length and breadth of the north of England. He would go, for example, to Morecambe for the day using nothing but public transport. It was, and still is, his escape from the stresses and strains of everyday life. He knows which type of bus is utilised for each route in his home town of Halifax, and he knows exactly what time the next bus will come along, and whether or not two or three will come along at once.

Eric Sykes' hobby is as therapeutic as mine, he does not need to share his passion with anyone else, although his friends and family are aware of it, and he is happy just doing what he is doing. This helps him to understand how I feel when I venture to the site of a long-forgotten football team for the first time. I suppose I also helped add an extra dimension to his hobby too – on more than one occasion he enquired as to the details of the well-enclosed, partially floodlit ground he could clearly see from public transport on the way to some far-flung destination.

Eric did once attend a convention of 'bus spotters' in his home town. He only went the once – he felt there were too many anoraks there! If only all headteachers possessed his sense of humour. He also wanted to write a book someday about the history of public transport in Calderdale – someone beat him too it, and what made it worse was that this person 'did a really good job of it, too'.

There are other anoraks who have been able to write as much as they want, whenever they want, for a living. I have met some of these people too. Whilst researching my slightly-less-than-best-selling histories of soccer in Keighley, I had to trawl through the sports pages of every single issue of the *Keighley News* and other long-gone local weeklies, going all the way back to the late 1800s. Local newspapers can be notoriously inconsistent and inaccurate in their coverage of local sports – more often than not depending on a large number of correspondents sending in reports and accounts pertaining to their own clubs, thereby lending themselves to a little biased reporting at times. On occasions I would encounter not only completely contradictory reports of the same game, but examples of different newspapers reporting completely different results for matches involving the same teams. Ingrow Celtic may have defeated Thwaites Brow 2-0 in an early twentieth century cup competition thanks to two well-taken goals according to one broadsheet, but the score was 1-1 in another.

The 1980s, however, were different. You really could rely on sports coverage in the *Keighley News*. This was due entirely to two anoraks, the newspaper's two sports editors during those times, Paul Jackson and Kevin Hopkinson. These two were different. They were anoraks themselves, not spotty know-alls who merely sat in their office and compiled the weekly facts and figures, but lads who were genuinely fanatical and passionate about every aspect of local sports. They not only wrote about sport, they took part in it too. They turned out for their local Sunday football team – Keighley News FC – in the Keighley Sunday Alliance. They would not only write the headlines, they would make the headlines – Hopkinson made the headlines when he was one of three members of the same family to score for his local village team, Bradley FC, in the same game. He still claims to this day that his strike was far sweeter than those scored by his son and his brother. But the real quality was in their writing. Not merely content with reporting on the previous week's events on the local sports fields, there would be previews of the following weekend's programme of events. They knew before anyone else that should Keighley Shamrocks win at home in the County Cup, it would mark their best run in the competition for over a decade – no-one at the club would have known that, but the Jacksons and Hopkinsons of this world did. They are perfect examples of the type of anorak you will find in the pub after the game, not alone in a dark corner but stood at the bar, getting the next round in.

So imagine the local sporting geek researching the history of his local sport in these very same pages of the *Keighley News*. Manna from heaven. If Jackson said it happened, it happened, exactly as he said it. If Hopkinson said it mattered, it really mattered. No need to double check results, no more sending off letters to request obscure final league tables – they were staring right at you in print. Of course Jackson and Hopkinson were anoraks, but for that decade even the Cross Hills Snooker League could not complain that local sport wasn't getting its fair share of coverage. It was Jackson who first penned a short history of soccer in Keighley. His account was serialised on the back page of the newspaper throughout the early 1980s. He was being paid for doing something that many of us do for hours upon end in our spare time, with no financial reward. I am sure that sitting in an upstairs office perusing past issues of the *Keighley News* was no great ordeal for this particular chap.

Kevin Hopkinson stepped into Jackson's shoes when the latter moved northwards in 1984 (to eventually work for

Dalesman publishing). Hopkinson himself moved to the position of sub-editor at the *Keighley News* in 1990. One of his roles then was to compile a series of 'Looking Back' pull-out sections that would inevitably ensure a little more advertising revenue for the newspaper's parent company – it will not surprise you to know that there was an awful lot of sport in this series. He also stepped back into his old shoes to cover for absences in the sports department – there it was like being back at home writing about his obsessions. Both refute claims that they are anoraks, though. 'We are just grumpy old men really,' claims Jackson. They may be grumpy old men, but they are anoraks too. The standard they set with their sports writing certainly had an influence on one future anorak back in the 1980s and '90s.

I am happy to say that I have met some delightfully pleasant anoraks over the years, whether groundhoppers of the 'Lost in Barrow' ilk, fanatical clubmen like Roy Mason and Tim Welsh, forum fanatics or specialists in the plethora of sporting facts and figures. They all love what they do, they take the inevitable criticism, but they are all perfectly sane individuals with perfectly normal social lives, and none of them would stand out in a crowd as being a little odd.

Chapter Nine

KEEPING IT REAL

There are many anoraks out there, but there are very few, if any, impostors. The advantage of living in the world of the obsessive is that this is not the type of thing where certain individuals want to jump on the bandwagon. There are very few fake anoraks. Who, after all, would want to make these claims unless they really had spent hours and hours researching local league tables or visiting obscure grounds. If you are wanting young women to throw their underwear in your direction then you are in the wrong place.

If there was to be a strange person who wanted to get in on the act in the world of the groundhopper or football statistician, they would be outed almost at once. They would be completely unaware of the lingo, and plainly unable to make a reasonable input into the vast array of specialised information on offer to the initiated on the day. You have to remember that an anorak will more than happily jump on even the slightest of inaccuracies, and will not let it go until his point has been well and truly exhausted.

A genuine anorak will spot the fake. Graham Souness should have consulted his local anoraks down on the South Coast when he was in charge at Southampton FC in November 1996. It would have saved many red faces at the club. The club took a telephone call purportedly from Liberian international and World Footballer of the Year George Weah, who recommended that they gave his good friend Ali Diah a trial. Little did they know that the gentleman on the other end of the line was, in fact, not Weah but Diah's agent, and that this supposedly fine sportsman was in reality a particularly poor football player. It was all a con. Somehow Diah managed to get on the bench for a league match against Leeds United, came on as substitute and was promptly withdrawn, but not before making an ass of himself and Southampton Football Club, and little was ever heard of him again. Rumour has it that this Senegalese gentleman returned to the slightly lesser surroundings of the non-League game in the north-east of England. Before returning to obscurity, he was reported as saying: 'I've been made to look a con man. It's just not true. I do know George Weah, but I'm certainly not his best mate. I employed an agent when I came to England and he is the con man. He must have been calling all these clubs pretending to be George.'

Any football statistician would have been able to see through this right from the start. Had Souness et al at Southampton announced Diah's imminent appearance beforehand someone would have pointed out that things were not quite as they seemed. How he managed to get himself on the substitutes' list for that game is equally as startling – had they not taken a look at him first? Mind you, those of us who witnessed

Bradford City's two glorious Premiership seasons would possibly argue that Bruno Rodriguez and Jorge Cadete were just as poor, if not worse, than Diah. But at least they had pedigree and had proved themselves in the years prior to their brief stints at Valley Parade, even if they lasted only a little longer at Bradford than the guy from Senegal did at Southampton.

There are the obvious name-droppers, who pretend to be friends with famous people. Geeks are not known for being gullible either. In the first place, they could probably make a far more convincing attempt at doing this than the name-dropper ever could.

The fake is not just confined to the likes of the impostor or the name-dropper, however. There is a plethora of fake sporting goods available on eBay and practically every other online auction site. Whether it be tickets, shirts, memorabilia or autographs, there are people out there selling not-so-honest items to an unsuspecting public. But the anorak knows best. For example, very few of us with unhealthy obsessions for seeking the truth about practically everything related to sport will be fooled by the fake Italian football shirts we could all so easily get hold of.

For a start, only a real idiot would be taken in by the low prices they are offered at – you just need a little bit of common sense for that – but there are also full-price fakes out there too. With any AS Roma shirt you should always check that they are ninety-two per cent polyester and eight per cent elastane, or eighty-eight per cent polyester and twelve per cent elastane. Never be fooled by the 100 per cent polyester shirt, especially if it is 'super fine quality polyester'. Polyester is polyester, it is all the same. Every anorak should know that.

163

Chapter Ten

ONWARD AND UPWARD

So how do you know if your partner is becoming an anorak? The chances are, he always has been, and you should jolly well have noticed before now. If not, then there are some tell-tale signs that should indicate a swing in that direction.

Be aware that shopping trips may well be the first indication. A trip to the local stationary store may result in the purchase of a small notebook or two, and a set of new biros. They may be stored in a safe place at home and there may be no reason offered for this. It may be pertinent to make a subtle query in this respect.

A trip to the nearest menswear shop may result in the purchase of a new raincoat. Now this is a giveaway, particularly if the garment is not of a leading market brand. Look out also for the new thermos flask that can be picked up in any cheap town-centre store, and even more cheaply in your nearest supermarket. Keep an eye on your Tupperware too.

Evenings in are not the same. Live televised games become even more boring. This is because your partner develops a tendency to declare that the commentator or expert summariser is wrong. He has erred in his delivery of the correct facts on the matter in question. Team X has not beaten team Y since 1967 – not 1968 as the expert has incorrectly told us. It becomes a little more unnerving when the person sat next to you on the couch starts to spew a whole host of historical and statistical information in your direction a good half-hour before John Motson does the same.

Inappropriate facts and figures begin to dominate your life, and at the most inappropriate times. Having mother for tea during a live televised match is akin to subjecting the poor lady to an array of absolutely irrelevant blurb relating to a team she is barely able to pronounce, never mind care about, and it is becoming harder and harder to encourage her to pop over every other Sunday.

Take note of the weekly mileage your spouse is covering. If he is becoming an anorak this figure should actually decrease – this is because he is making greater use of public transport to get around. Train timetables could well indicate that he has begun to groundhop. Be aware. There may also be an increasing number of subscription-only magazines popping through your letter-box, a simple chat with the postman may confirm your suspicions.

Watch out for the tell-tale signs during your evenings out together. A sudden, previously unheard-of urge to take part in the pub quiz may be encountered. A blinding rage when the question master actually gets one of his own questions wrong is another sign. It would not be a pub quiz if there wasn't some cock-up somewhere, but it is only the anorak who will not accept anything but the correct answer.

Don't think that going abroad will be any cure for his behaviour. It may exacerbate the problem. Before you depart, he may wish to fully research the history of his favourite sport in your chosen destination. Once there, he may go in search of football grounds, and he may do this subtly. There may be ulterior motives for his desire to go on a long romantic walk or a drive into the countryside in a hire car. His idea of fun may be very different to what you are expecting. If he does happen to stumble across a football ground (the map he is carrying could be a giveaway, look carefully at where the ink marks are that he made), he will wish to return to that same place should there be an impending match to be played there. Remember that some countries have their domestic fixtures during the British holiday season. He will also want a match-day programme and will undoubtedly stumble across a foreign language book detailing the entire history of all manner of sports in that country.

So, if your spouse is displaying all or some of these tell-tale signs, what should you do? Should you seek the advice of family members, or a marriage guidance councillor? Is this grounds for divorce? Absolutely not. This is not an illness, it is merely obsessive interest. It is not illegal. Should your teenage son show these symptoms then thank your lucky stars that he is not roaming the streets every night or glue sniffing. You may even come to recognise the previously unheard-of places that are suddenly thrown in your direction, and you may grow to understand and love his new friends as much as he does. Your groundhopper of a husband might hang around with people who spend all day talking about and looking for football grounds, but at least he is not knocking off that floozy who lives at the end of the street – now that would be grounds for divorce. You are going to have to get used to it. Mrs Grillo has certainly got used to it.

The anorak will live forever, hopefully. There will always be final tables to compile in May, or in the autumn when the cricket season is complete. New clubs will always emerge, others will fall by the wayside, grounds will be built over, and leagues will amalgamate. This needs documenting, someone will want to know all about them some time in the future – and even if they don't, the anorak wants to know about it right now.

For me, there will always be the Keighley & District FA Cup final, as well as other key end-of-season 'must-dos' such as the Keighley Sunday Cup and Keighley Supplementary Cup finals. They will always need documenting; December will always be a difficult month to negotiate. I must organise my Christmas and New Year programme with care, making great efforts not to upset the wife, or the in-laws. Football matches must not clash with family responsibilities. I really hope the latest Human League gig will not clash with a Silsden home fixture. Annual holidays in August always present a dilemma – the early rounds of the FA Cup are in August. Therefore, should I make that journey to the north-east to see Silsden in action in an extra preliminary-round tie or should I set off to northern Scotland on time with Mrs Grillo? Scenario one is usually considered, but on pain of death not followed through – the boss does get her own way once a year, and at least I have the Lost in Barrow clan on hand, keeping me informed, via text message, of the major talking points at the big match.

As a schoolteacher, I also have to contend with similar situations where a parents' evening, or some other such obligation, clashes with a key midweek football fixture. You'll appreciate that this is about as welcome as a cockroach in my salad. I could be on the road to Ramsbottom instead, or down the road at Cougar Park. I have been known to sneak out of some events early without being detected, and I now have to recycle my excuses for not making appointments after 7.15p.m. Among my proudest moments thus far: 'The cat has been run over, it is having a major operation to save it's back end' (strictly speaking this story is true, although it happened two years before I first made that particular excuse), 'Mrs G is in hospital as she is a tad unwell' (she was due to have a small operation the following week), and 'I am going stewarding' (i.e. I am off early in order to sell a few raffle tickets at the Silsden match, which kicks off in little over half an hour). Illness has been faked on more than one occasion. As my current boss is unlikely to ever read this, I like to think that some of these rather lame excuses could be recycled for a little longer.

It is also very likely that at a parents' evening a rather disgruntled parent will accost me. This has happened before. Despite appreciating my value as a professional, this particular individual will be unable to forgive me for awarding, in one of my books, his sensational match-winning goal in some league cup final to a player who had not even played in said tie. 'Oh, so you're Mr Grillo are you?' will precede the sentence that begins 'I was reading your book the other day and I noticed…'

Well I can tell you that following extensive research, Black Horse (formerly Royal FC) were indeed thrown out of the Wharfedale Sunday league in 1989, they did not jump before they were pushed. I don't care how many parents disagree with this, even if they were stalwarts of this infamous local side. I am an anorak; I know my stuff.

In recent years, researching the history of a particular football league or club is made that bit easier by the information that has been posted on the internet. If you can't locate the information you need then you can be sure that there is someone you can readily contact who may be able to help you. Email can be a man's best friend these days. Those rare books that were previously the speciality of the back-street shop are much more easily unearthed these days – bad news for the bookshop but a lot easier for the customer. It does mean that a rare bargain will no longer be a true bargain any more – with countless other anoraks watching the same item on eBay, you are more likely to have to pay something like its true market price, but at least you have a better chance of locating that copy at the other side of the country.

Age does not seem to be holding me, or others, back. I have often wondered where my future as a sad statto or obsessive compulsive lies. Where do I go from here? How long can I go on for? Will I always be obsessed with the compilation of every single final football table in the history of mankind – even when I am ninety-five? Will I always have the desire to do that extra bit of research into one of the most obscure and little-talked-about local sides from the local Sunday league? Again, the internet has made things like this more simple – easier to locate that one league or club official who might have a record of those missing facts are historical sites and, of course, the forums where one is able to request or share information with like-minded individuals.

So for how long will I be a regular and resident anorak – albeit not the only resident anorak – down at Silsden Football Club? It is not inconceivable that the club could fold through lack of finance, slip back into local football or merge with another, bigger club. I pray that none of these scenarios will ever be played out, but for someone who has written about and followed the lack of success of Keighley football over the years, it would not be the biggest shock to the system (I really do hope they will continue to rise up the leagues). Whatever would I do if a new Keighley Town were to emerge from the shadows, take on the mantle of top local side and blast their way upwards through the football pyramid, into the Football League and even the Premiership? The idea is hardly worth a visit to William Hill, but stranger things have surely happened somewhere.

If you think about it, should any of this happen then I will still be an anorak. Changing circumstances will not see the decline of the anorak. For instance, Grillo's Gallopers (of my Subbuteo and Recitel football game days) have recently been revived. They have transmogrified into AFC Grillo and they compete remarkably unsuccessfully in the many fantasy football leagues that exist in this day and age.

Surely Subbuteo will always be around too. A study, completed in 2002, suggested that over ninety per cent of fathers over the age of thirty had played or owned the game in their youth. Even now there are table-football competitions scattered around Britain. American giants Hasbro may not be particularly interested in the Subbuteo brand they current own, but there are still enthusiasts out there, and not all of them are the wrong side of forty. Who said that computer games had killed the real thing? Peter Adolph's 1947 invention could knock the spots off everything we see on the toy shelves these days.

There will always be information to unearth, facts, figures and rare pressings to collect. The world evolves, and so does that way you research or gather your information. With the whole world being opened up to us through these new forms of electronic media, it surely gives more scope for the potential anorak. It may be that there are more anoraks about, or that it is harder to actually unearth something that nobody else ever knew, or linked together, but there is plenty of scope for the average statto to jump headlong into something that will bring very little in the way of material rewards but much in the way of private pleasures.

As I put the finishing touches to this book, there are more and more facts and figures that need looking into. The Huddersfield Works and Combination League has reverted back to two divisions; the Sheffield Sports and Wharfedale Sunday football leagues appear to have become defunct; there seem to be two different East Leeds teams in two different leagues; Pellon United and Old Almondburians have folded; and, best of all, Silsden reserves have shifted across from the East Lancashire League to the Harrogate League (not bad for a club which is located neither in Lancashire nor the Harrogate district). All of this needs investigating further, there is no stone to be left unturned in seeking out every detail, every what, where, or how in local football.

If, then, I finally achieve my ambition of collecting every single final league table from the world of association football, and finally run out of defunct football grounds to locate, then I can always retire with my trusty three-quarter-length quilted anorak, with soft raccoon trim that adorns the detachable down-filled hood (it sure beats the tactel plain-dyed water-repellent one with 100 per cent poly-mesh lining I saw earlier). That, I fear, will never happen.

DIARY OF AN ANORAK

In the world of this particular anorak – and upon completion of the day job – an average day will involve one, some or all of the following (and in any order):

Check email
Check eBay – bid when appropriate
Peruse and, if necessary, post on Silsden FC forum
Peruse/post on other sporting forums, including those of Tony Kempster and The Fellrunners' Association
Go for a run
Write an article (or book)
Read an article (book, magazine or website)
Do a spot of research from a variety of sources
Go and watch a football match (or at least watch one on TV)
Spend some quality time with Mrs Grillo

Therefore, there is something of a routine each day. I must stress that weekends will also involve completion of many of the above tasks, as well as fulfilling one's social life. One has been known to go out on with the lads on a Thursday or Friday night too.

Each month, however, brings with it a unique set of experiences or tasks that must be completed – or at least attempted. Below is just a flavour of what each may entail:

August

Of course, January is the first month of the year, but not for this sporting geek. This month signals the beginning of the football season.

Ensure Silsden FC season ticket is purchased before first home game of the season, and before the annual fortnight's holiday to some far-flung destination, or closer to home in the highlands of Scotland.

Once on holiday, seek out previously uncharted football grounds. Easy excuse: 'I'm just off for a run.' Works on most occasions.

Back home: confirm, and then reconfirm, the composition of the myriad of local sporting competitions. Stay calm as everything is thrown into confusion when Ring O Bells (Shipley) withdraw from one league, reform and join a rival competition, decide to merge with another club from the village, and then decide to disband altogether at the last minute. All of this has to be meticulously recorded.

Try to visit as many lost grounds as possible – either during the week (remember, school's out for summer), or en-route to Silsden away fixture.

Ensure that all local cricket final tables are collated, as well as those from the Australian soccer leagues. Oh, and the rugby league ones from the Summer Conference leagues. I always forget those.

Be careful not to fall for claims that local press will be downsizing its sports pages, and make sure you check with editor of said newspaper before repeating these rumours to others.

September

Wedding anniversary this month. If this falls on a Saturday then very problematic.

Early rounds of FA competitions to fit in. Therefore new destinations – a trip to Darlington or the east coast for instance. Make sure that the Robinson clan are fully primed on exact route to destination and that sat nav is turned on.

Midweek fixtures galore. Ditto above comment re. the Robinsons.

Birthday at end of month. Create space in loft for football trivia books. Best place is the space behind important magazines, both past and present, such as *Non-League Retrospect*, *Groundtastic*, *Non-League Traveller*, *Bureau of Non-League Football* and *Pyramid*.

Organise school fantasy football competition. Pin up Steeton FC posters around school building – their manager is on the lookout for hot new talent.

Apologise profusely to editor of local newspaper for furthering the rumours that sports pages will be downsized.

October

Strong possibility that Silsden have been forced to concentrate on league and County Cup only by now. If still in national competitions then season will be reaching fever pitch.

First week of month, remember to take unwanted trivia books received as birthday presents to OXFAM or other charity shop.

First school holiday of the academic year. Delay jobs around the house that have been put off in order to fully update and reorganise league composition records, and to peruse some of the domestic, European and world football annuals that have been published over the past few weeks.

November

Shiny new anorak needed – weather deteriorating. Wife suspects that I am 'playing away' as 'nobody in their right mind would want to go and watch a football match in this weather'. I would. So would Pete Hanson and John Barclay, and the Robinsons.

Important changes to school fantasy football team to be made. Bottom position is not acceptable when you are the resident anorak.

Pin up newly designed Steeton FC posters. They are top of the league but Roy Mason would still welcome hot new talent at Summerhill Lane.

Purchase Atherton Laburnum Rovers match-day programme at their home fixture with Silsden.

Congratulate Ian and Ronnie Wharton on their 100th game of the season.

December

Create space in loft for expected football trivia books before Christmas day.

Finish reading Atherton Laburnum Rovers programme, possibly around end of second week in month.

Boxing Day fixtures are the source of much disharmony. Silsden away from home at the other side of Manchester – must be back in time for tea. Mother-in-law has been invited. Busy schedule in Football League – thus allowing me the opportunity to attend Bradford City home fixture. Purchase of *The City Gent* fanzine – essential. Return home and write article for next issue of above fanzine.

January

First week of month, remember to take unwanted trivia books received as Christmas presents to OXFAM or other charity shop.

Declare that fantasy football is a game of chance and that anyone can do it. After all, that is why a year seven girl with no knowledge of sport whatsoever is top of the school table and I am one off the bottom.

Due to inclement weather, longest away trips with Silsden FC usually result in cancellation of fixture at last minute. Therefore waste of a 150-plus-mile round trip. I sulk. The wife gets cross. Potential marital disharmony.

February

'Parents' day at Steeton FC' fliers to distribute around school.

February half-term holiday results in the undertaking of essential local rugby history research at Keighley library. Therefore, household chores put on hold until next holiday. Missing information may also result in a visit to Bradford library.

Further inclement weather results in cancellation of all local sporting fixtures and household tasks finally being completed (well, partially).

Dearth of midweek fixtures enables one to make inroads into the substantial pile of publications that need to be read. Alternatively, make a few extra visits to sunny Todmorden, the home of Border Bookshop (drop wife off at garden centre on the way).

March

Make the bold decision to take in as many County Amateur League fixtures as possible before end of season. This is due to the fact that local teams are all vying for promotion.

Major disruption to the sporting calendar as another week-long trip to Scotland is undertaken, right at the end of the month. Destination is the Isle of Arran as usual. The only local potential fixture will probably involve the Lamlash versus Arran Veterans fixture. Free entry but, alas, not a cat in hell's chance of a match-day programme.

As evenings begin to get lighter, arrange more off-road runs with Chris Tordoff. Woe betide any local farmer who may wish to slyly close off any public rights of way. We are coming to get you!

April

Attempt to limit number of County Amateur League fixtures attended due to 'gentle persuasion' from the wife. Silsden have a huge backlog of games to fit in this month, and their academy side have key fixtures, and the reserves are still in the cup.

Reply to emails from Roy Mason regarding possible Steeton FC players at school.

Congratulate Ian and Ronnie Wharton on their 300th game of the season.

May

Cup finals month: Keighley Cups (x3), County Cup competitions, Craven & District League Northern Plant Hire Trophy, Keighley and Aire Valley Sunday Alliance Jeff Hall Trophy, and many more. All involve local sides and it is only right that all are attended.

Play-offs and final league fixtures to fit in also. A busy month – watertight excuses utilised for the skipping of staff meetings, parents' evenings and the like. All fixtures play havoc with extra GCSE revision classes.

Final league tables to compile. This takes time too.

Cricket season begins. Not really my scene but nevertheless league compositions to record, as well as progress of my local team – based right on top of one of the most exposed hills in the village – who are struggling for numbers.

Australian league soccer: league compositions, name changes, merger to consider.

Congratulate Ian and Ronnie Wharton on their 350th game of the season.

June

Three months off domestic football. Almost. There is always the summer Strathspey and Badenoch Welfare League north of the border, and one or two obscure Welsh competitions I could fit in. There's also the Intertoto Cup.

Articles to compose: Silsden FC fanzine, *City Gent*, *Non-League Retrospect* and the like. What can I write that I haven't bored everybody with already?

Begrudgingly distribute school fantasy football trophies. Devise a way of awarding the gentleman who finished eleventh in the staff league table, and forty-fifth (out of forty-seven) overall, a medal.

July

During particularly fine weather, make bold decision to take part in village gala fell race. After all, it's only five miles and involves far less climbing than many.

An exciting month: FA Cup, Trophy and Vase draws published. Who will Silsden draw? FA Youth Cup and Sunday Cup competitions also published. Silsden are in these too. Oh, what an exciting season ahead.

Regular visits to Tony Kempster's forum are a must – all the hot news will be posted there first.

James Wright publishes his *Non-League Newsdesk Annual*. The bible. Essential reading at bath time, bedtime and staff meetings.

Re-retire from all means of competitive fell running following abject performance in local fell race – my most embarrassing performance since being overtaken by Tigger the Tiger in previous year's Great North Run.

THE ANORAK'S GUIDE TO THE ENGLISH FOOTBALL PYRAMID

Until the late 1970s leagues popped up all over the place, some were stronger than others, some lasted only a season or two and others were breakaway organisations formed by disenchanted clubs who wanted a change or better competition.

In 1979 the Football Association assisted in the formation of the Alliance Premier League, made up of the best non-League clubs in the country. Within a few years, automatic promotion to the Football League was guaranteed every season, replacing the old end-of-season election system, whereby the top non-League clubs would usually see their aspirations thwarted. The Alliance Premier has since been known as the Conference and has recently been renamed the Blue Square Premier, following a new sponsorship deal. This is known as 'step one'.

Below this there have been many changes over the years, but as it stands now there are two leagues feeding into the Conference: the Conference North and Conference South, both formed in 2004. These are therefore known as 'step two'.

Below these there are three 'step three' leagues: the Northern Premier (formed in 1968), Southern (formed 1894) and Isthmian (formed 1905) Leagues. These have had various name changes recently due to sponsorship deals, and this is where the problems start. The boundaries of the Southern and Isthmian Leagues traditionally overlapped because the Southern League catered for ambitious professional teams that wanted to get into the big time, while the Isthmian was for many years an amateur league, although its clubs were of an equal standing with those of the Southern and Northern Premier Leagues. The FA has spent a good deal of time negotiating with those involved and, not without a fair few problems, has managed to simplify things somewhat. Therefore, the Isthmian League is now more orientated towards the Home Counties than the Southern League.

'Step four' consists of two regional second divisions of the above premier leagues, making six divisions in all. They are: Southern League Division One 'South and East' and 'Midlands', Isthmian League Division One 'North' and 'South', and Northern Premier League Division One 'North' and 'South', the latter two formed as recently as summer 2007.

There are many more leagues at 'step five', some of which contain lower divisions, which are at 'step six' and below. It all depends of the status of their member's grounds and playing standards. Below these are the hundreds of local and regional leagues, some of which are pyramid feeder leagues. The FA will no doubt incorporate them all over the next few years.

Step five leagues that feed into the Northern Premier league are: North West Counties League, Northern Counties East league and Northern League. Those that feed into the

Southern League are: Midland Alliance (which could become a feeder to the Northern Premier soon, and which is itself fed into by the Midland Combination and West Midlands Regional League), Western League, Eastern Counties League, Hellenic League, Kent League, Wessex League and United Counties League. Isthmian League feeders are: Essex Senior League, Combined Counties League and Spartan South Midlands League.

Since the pyramid is being reorganised as we speak, changes over the next few years are inevitable, and clubs can be moved around into parallel leagues in order to keep numbers equal. The average football anorak will be able to discuss these issues at length and to keep totally up to date with it all – Tony Kempster's website really is worth perusing.

THE ANORAK'S GUIDE TO THE SCOTTISH FOOTBALL PYRAMID

The Scottish League is a closed shop. There are not many of those left these days. Successful non-League clubs can only enter the Scottish League if there is a vacancy. Although there are far fewer teams in Scotland than there are in England, there is no official pyramid in place yet. This is because factions within the game kept falling out with each other and thus formed separate governing bodies.

At non-League level there are three senior competitions, whose fifty-odd teams are able to enter the Scottish Cup, and the Highland, East of Scotland and South of Scotland Leagues. Below these are the amateur leagues, based mainly around the major urban areas.

There is also a Scottish Junior FA, comprising 160 or so clubs. The term 'junior' applies to status rather than age. Junior teams have traditionally been unable to enter the Scottish FA Cup, but this hasn't prevented many of them attracting larger crowds than several Scottish League teams, and organising their own highly successful cup competition. The top junior leagues are easily on a par with the Highland, South and

East of Scotland Leagues. In recent times a pyramid structure has been developed in the junior ranks, based around three regions.

The west region has Premier and Division One sections, the latter being fed by the Ayrshire and Central Leagues. The east region comprises two top divisions – Super League and Premier League – which serves three lower competitions – North, Central and South Divisions. In the north there are fewer clubs, with a much more straightforward three-division structure. There has been talk of uniting all these competitions into one all-embracing Scottish pyramid; however, talk is all it is at the moment.

THE ANORAK'S GUIDE TO THE WELSH FOOTBALL PYRAMID

The problem with football in Wales is that the north and south have always been separate entities, and many clubs prefer to direct their allegiances to the English FA. There have been several attempts at forming a Welsh National League, the latest in 1992 following pressure from UEFA, Europe's ruling body. Unfortunately, chaos ensued. At the same time the Welsh FA insisted that all clubs playing in the English non-League pyramid must return to Welsh competition, with the exception of Merthyr Tydfil, who harboured aspirations to play in the Football League. Many of these clubs refused and so were banned for playing at their home grounds in Wales. Despite having played in English competitions since time began, the likes of Newport County, Barry Town and Caernarfon Town were therefore all exiled until the Welsh FA changed their minds. Then, in an act that smacked of double standards, the Welsh FA allowed an English team, Oswestry Town, to play in a Welsh competition because they 'always have done'. No they haven't.

The competition that is now known as the Welsh Premier League has two feeder leagues: the Cymru Alliance in the north of the Principality, and the three-division Welsh League in the south. The Cymru Alliance has two other leagues feeding into it: the Welsh Alliance and the Welsh National (Wrexham Area) League. The southern-based Welsh League is fed by the South Wales Senior and South Wales Amateur Leagues, along with other competitions such as the Gwent and Neath Leagues. There are various other local and regional competitions such as the Mid-Wales and Swansea Senior Leagues that provide teams for higher competitions.

The main benefit of the formation of a new national league for Wales would be entry into European competition for its champion club.

FURTHER READING

Any reading is further reading for the anorak. All of the titles mentioned in this book are worth reading, although most are not available on the shelves of WHSmith, so you may have to dig a little deeper if you wish to collect some or all of them.

If you have to begin somewhere, then look no further than the British Library, which has published three of the essential items any master of statistics should own. *The Football Compendium*, *The Athletics Compendium* and *The Rugby Compendium* contain details of every book written on these respective sports. Yes, three books that contain details about books. Once in your hands, the world is your oyster.

With club histories (of any sport), the general rule of thumb is that the smaller the team being written about then the more specialised the book, and the more likely it is to be bought by the average statto. The same applies to any league or cup competition being written about. The most expensive books are not necessarily the most informative, so beware of gloss and dross.

If you want a little bit more about the world of geeky pastimes, then you can check out *Fotheringham's Extraordinary Sporting Pastimes* (Robson Books, 2006). Plenty of geeks to read about in this book, which will raise more than the occasional chuckle from anyone with a sense of humour.

Also by Rob Grillo – books for anoraks, written by an anorak: *Chasing Glory* and *Glory Denied* (Empire Publications, 1998 and 1999); *The Story of Association Football in Keighley*, volumes one and two; *Staying the Distance* (1999); *100 Years On – The First Bradford City FC, the Early Years of Bradford (Park Avenue) and Other Stories* (Parrs Wood Press, 2001).

Log on to www.anoraknophobia.co.uk

Or www.myspace.com/anoraknophobiabook